Beat the
BORDER

04 AUG 95

For Tom Banchich,
magister optimus

Matthew C. Riley
(a.k.a. Neil
Beaumont)

Beat the BORDER

AN INSIDER'S GUIDE TO HOW THE U.S. BORDER WORKS & HOW TO BEAT IT

NED BEAUMONT

PALADIN PRESS ■ BOULDER, COLORADO

Beat the Border:
An Insider's Guide to How the U.S. Border Works and How to Beat It
by Ned Beaumont

Copyright © 1995 by Ned Beaumont

ISBN 0-87364-833-1
Printed in the United States of America

Published by Paladin Press, a division of
Paladin Enterprises, Inc., P.O. Box 1307,
Boulder, Colorado 80306, USA.
(303) 443-7250

Direct inquiries and/or orders to the above address.

CONTENTS

v

INTRODUCTION

"multa cum libertate notabant"

—Horace, *Sermones* 1.4.5

Free men want to travel freely. In today's world of big, bureaucratic states, however, border guards and complex regulations often impede free travel. Such impediments to human liberty are even in place in that "land of the free," the United States of America.

Crossing the U.S. border can be a trial no matter how honest and law-abiding a man may be. The desperate and the criminal have the option of illegal entry, sneaking across the American border at the empty spaces of the desert or along the rocky coast. Most travelers, though, attempt to cross at lawful points of entry.

This book is for them.

Every time they try to cross the border into the United States, they are subject to inspection by a uniformed officer of the government. Every year, thousands of those people are denied admission to the U.S.—often for trivial, purely technical, or easily avoidable reasons.

This book will teach you to avoid those problems.

Why follow my advice? Because I have been and I have done.

As a U.S. Immigration Inspector, I guarded the border. Along the way, I learned and used all the tricks—legal, extralegal, and downright dirty—that inspectors use to keep people from crossing. I saw the ways people inadvertently kept themselves from crossing. I came to know the difference between the border as it is supposed to work and the way it really works.

Now you can know all that, too. No longer need you worry about being stalled or stopped at the border. With an insider's knowledge, you can beat the border.

INSPECTION

What Is It?

Every time you cross the border into the United States—from north or south, from east coast or west—you are going to be inspected.

Inspected? Me? Inspected?

Yes, you. Unless, of course, you sneak across the border. But anytime you cross the border *legally*, you are going to get inspected.

Inspected.

That has a nasty ring to it. Perhaps you have never crossed the border and experienced inspection. Perhaps you have crossed the border and didn't even realize you were being inspected. Perhaps you read the sign at the border checkpoint ("Stop For Government Inspection") but never really thought about the questions you answered as an inspection.

If you did think about that word "inspection," then you may

have been apprehensive, even scared. Or you may have been angry. You wouldn't be alone.

A PIECE OF MEAT

I was just a beginning inspector, working for the Immigration and Naturalization Service (INS). I'd been doing inspections in a booth by myself ("on the line" in the jargon of the trade) at a major international airport for less than a week. It was summer vacation time, and therefore also summer travel time. The planes were packed and the airport was crowded. Every booth was open and manned. There were long lines of hot, tired, and frustrated people.

A short, bald man with a face like a well-used catcher's mitt and a thick New York accent stepped into my booth.

I began the usual commands and questions: "Let me have your boarding pass and identification, please." "What is your citizenship?" "Where were you born?" "How long have you been outside of the United States?"

Most of those questions were unnecessary. But I was still green.

Well, the New Yorker must have been late for his flight. And he was the sort of character who thrives in the Big Apple: always in a hurry and unwilling to be slowed down. He answered the first three questions. The fourth was too much.

"Why are you asking me all these questions?"

"Sir,"—I was still polite in those days—"you have to be inspected like everyone else."

I'd said the dirty word. "Inspected?" he shouted, full of indignation. "Inspected?" He was incredulous. "What am I? A piece of meat?"

He had a point.

EQUAL OPPORTUNITY INSPECTION

No matter what that man thought—or what you may think—the fact remains that unless you cross the border illegally, you are going to get inspected. There's no way around it. That's the way the law is written: *everyone* gets inspected. Everyone includes U.S. citizens and visitors from foreign countries, babies and nonagenarians, congressmen, senators, and even the president.

Never, ever, think that you are being singled out for some special harassment when an inspector questions you. He questions everyone.

The Number One Rule of the border is simply this: EVERYONE GETS INSPECTED.

As a consequence, the Number One Rule for you as a border-crosser is: don't think that you are a target of special discrimination because you are being inspected. When an inspector decides to harass you, believe me, you'll know it.

WHERE TO EXPECT INSPECTION

Now that you understand that everyone gets inspected, you need to know where to expect inspection. Some of the inspection stations might surprise you.

"Well, you're wrong there, Mr. Know-it-all Inspector," you may be thinking. "It's easy to know where to expect a border inspection. At the border."

Ah, but there I have you. For the purposes of government inspection, "the border" can be hundreds, even thousands, of miles from the real borders of the United States.

Of course, one place where you'll face inspection *is* just where you'd expect. And that is at the border—either at the southern border with Mexico or at the northern border with Canada. If you've visited El Paso, you may have crossed the Rio Grande for some local color and bargain shopping in Juarez. When you came back across the bridge, you were inspected. If you came to see one of the Natural Wonders of the World in Niagara Falls, New York, you probably heard that the view of the Canadian falls in Niagara Falls, Ontario, was better (it is, by the way). So you took the Rainbow Bridge into Canada. When you recrossed the bridge into the United States, you were inspected. There was no surprise in either case. You were at the border, and that's where you'd expect a border inspection.

Unless you're in the Merchant Marine, it's unlikely that you've faced inspection at one of America's seaports, such as San Francisco, New Orleans, or New York City. The seashore, however, is the border of the U.S. (really the three-mile limit, I suppose, but that's the Coast Guard's bailiwick). You should expect to find uniformed inspectors ready to meet you when you get off the ship. But, except for short cruises, most of us don't do much sea travel and so don't have much experience of being inspected at seaports.

Instead of ship travel, however, we routinely travel by air. At airports you are very likely to face inspection—even though the airport isn't anywhere near the actual geographic borders of the United States.

Inspections, therefore, may take place at inland airports where planes first land in the U.S. For purposes of the INS and the Customs Service, international airports in such places as Chicago, Las Vegas, and Dallas are the U.S. "border." Don't be surprised just because those places are hundreds of miles from Mexico and Canada.

Even if inspectors at such inland airports aren't news to you (they do make a certain logical sense), you may be surprised to find that immigration and customs inspections at the U.S. "border" can take place outside the United States. In fact, U.S. inspectors work in countries other than the United States, being stationed at select international airports. This is what is called "preflight inspection" because inspectors try to catch you before you board your plane. Check your passport for INS stamps with "PFI"—the abbreviation used for the preflight system.

Preflight inspection is the wave of the future. The airlines and the U.S. government both like the system because it saves time and money. It saves time by reducing the long lines and longer waits at Customs and Immigration inspection booths at large U.S. airports, such as JFK in New York and LAX in Los Angeles. It saves money by stopping those persons who are excludable from the U.S. in foreign countries so that they never even get aboard a U.S.-bound plane. Thereby, the government doesn't have to pay for detention and deportation. That means more tax money for congressmen to go on "fact-finding" tours of resort beaches in the Caribbean.

Preflight inspection ports are found in countries that are both friendly to the United States government and send many travelers to the U.S. In other words, you're not going to find preflight inspection in Baghdad or Pyongyang.

If you stop and think about it for a moment, the obvious candidate for PFI stations is Canada. Canada is the immediate neighbor of the United States, shares the longest undefended border in the world with the U.S. (there hasn't been a war on our northern border since Napoleon was still in power), and is America's largest trading partner. Canada is also cold, so thousands of Canadian "snowbirds" flock to Florida and other warm-weather tourist havens every year. As a result, there are preflight inspection stations at airports in many large Canadian cities, such as Montreal, Toronto, Calgary, and Vancouver. If you're getting on a flight to Miami at Pearson Airport in Toronto, don't be surprised when you have to talk to U.S. Immigration before you board the plane.

Other preflight ports are located in Europe. A major one is located at Shannon Airport in Ireland. On a trial basis, the system has been used for U.S.-bound flights from London, England, and Frankfurt, Germany. Some countries are touchy about having their own citizens turned away by representatives of the U.S. government on their own soil. However, since preflight inspection saves time and money, expect to see it soon in places like Amsterdam, Paris, and Tokyo. Maybe even Mexico City will become a PFI port because of NAFTA. When there's a preflight in Libya, I'll be surprised.

PRIMARY VS. SECONDARY INSPECTION

There are two levels of inspection: primary and secondary. It is possible to face primary and secondary inspection from both Immigration and Customs; that is, you can be inspected four times at one crossing. In most cases, however, you'll face only primary inspection from either a Customs or Immigration inspector.

By using the techniques and applying the information contained in this book, you will be better able to avoid secondary inspection. Thereby, you will cross the border more easily and more quickly.

Primary Inspection

Most inspections are primary inspections. They take place "on the line," or in the rows of booths at bridges, roadways, and airports. They're routine for the inspectors and should become routine for you. Primary inspections are nothing to get excited about.

Primary inspections are short. They usually last from 30 to 60 seconds per person inspected. The rule of thumb I was taught when I was a beginning inspector was this:

If the inspection was taking longer than a minute, it was time to send the alien to secondary. During especially busy times at busy border crossings, primary inspections might run very much faster than a minute. Fifteen to twenty seconds is more typical during the summer at places like El Paso and Niagara Falls.

Inspectors are instructed by their bosses and by the training manuals to take as much time as is necessary to complete a thorough, by-the-book inspection. And, indeed, an inspector will take as much time as he needs if he suspects some real criminal or serious exclusion. Why not? He's paid by the hour, not the inspection.

But in practical terms, most primary inspections remain quite short because most travelers are legitimate tourists or businessmen fully admissible under the law. The inspector can complete those inspections in a minute. Moreover, the pressures of crowds and the influences of other inspectors on the line—who are anxious that each inspector take care of his fair share of the traveling public—will tend to speed up inspections during busy times and slow them down during slack times. A good general rule, but not an ironclad one, is that if your primary inspection is taking more than a minute, the inspector is setting you up for secondary.

Slow inspectors soon develop bad reputations among their fellows. Good inspectors don't like to work with slowpokes. Can you blame them? Would you want to handle half of your co-worker's job for no extra pay?

A glance at a typical (as much as any inspection can be "typical") primary inspection indicates just how quick, simple, and easy they are.

Let's say that you're a citizen of the United States who was born in the U.S. (from my experience, that's the case with the vast majority of inspections). You've driven across the Rio Grande to see El Paso from the Mexican side. You spent the afternoon in Mexico, took in the sights, and bought a few postcards as souvenirs. Now you're driving back across the bridge into the U.S.

You stop beside one of a row of booths. An Immigration Inspector there says, "What's your citizenship?"

"United States," you answer.

"Did you buy anything in Mexico?"

"Just some postcards."

"Okay, go ahead."

And that's it. You drive away. Quick, easy, and simple.

That inspection could, of course, have had a hundred or more variations. The inspector might ask where you were born. He might ask for identification, then type your name into his computer. He might ask you to step out of your car and open the trunk. Still, the typical primary inspection is going to be painless and short. It will last a minute or less.

If I had a dollar for every inspection I conducted that ran pretty much like the hypothetical one I described, I could buy my own country and never have to bother with borders.

Secondary Inspection

After a primary inspection, the inspector may still have doubts about whether you are admissible to the U.S. under the law. In that case, he will send you for a secondary inspection.

Note well my use of the phrase "admissible under the law." Inspectors can and will send you to secondary just to give you a hard time (if you create problems for them), but that's uncommon. In almost every case, when you are sent to secondary, the inspector is not singling you out because of some personal animosity toward you. He is sending you to secondary because his job is to enforce the law. And the law may say that you need to fill out a form or pay a fee or have your passport stamped before you can legally enter the United States. In most cases, secondary inspection is no more reason to worry than is primary inspection. In other words, no reason at all.

Both U.S. Customs and the INS conduct secondary inspections. Usually you'll be sent to one or the other. Sometimes, especially if you're suspected of being a criminal or a smuggler, you'll face secondary inspections from both Customs and Immigration.

The Customs Service is an arm of the Department of the Treasury, so its concern is with goods and money. Like another arm of the Treasury, the Internal Revenue Service (IRS), the job of the Customs Service involves taking your money and giving it to the U.S. government.

Customs secondary inspection can involve searches and interrogation. More often it involves merely filling out some forms (such as the ubiquitous customs declaration) and paying a tax on some goods purchased in a foreign country. The taxes collected by the Customs Service are called "duties," but they're still taxes.

If an inspector asks you if you have any "dutiable goods," he's asking about what you bought outside the U.S. A good general rule is to expect to be charged duty—and therefore be sent to Customs secondary—if you bought a lot of anything or any substantial amounts of alcohol or tobacco. Customs inspectors don't like to bother with the small stuff. When I was starting out on the land border, a Customs Inspector told me to never send in a secondary for five or ten dollars of duty. "If it won't pay for the paperwork," he said, "don't send it in."

Immigration secondary also tends to be simple. The most common reason for sending a traveler to INS secondary concerns documentary requirements (filling out a form) and/or having those forms or your passport stamped. Chapter 10 contains a discussion of INS documents.

If you're not sent to INS secondary because of documents, you'll probably be sent for more in-depth questioning. Now, "in-depth questioning" may give you visions of Resistance heroes caught in the clutches of the Gestapo, but on the U.S. border such questioning is rarely cause for concern.

Remember when I said that primary inspections are almost always limited to a minute or less? And remember that I also said that subtle (and sometimes not-so-subtle) pressure from colleagues causes an inspector to keep his inspections short? Well, that need to keep primary inspections brief is what leads to many secondary inspections. If, for whatever reason, an inspector cannot determine if you're admissible under the law with just a few questions and within about a minute, he'll send you to secondary.

Most of these type of secondaries arise because of minor miscommunications. INS and Customs inspectors learn Spanish as part of their jobs, because Mexico is the largest source of illegal immigration. Both services also like to employ people who have at least a smattering of some other language. Therefore, you'll frequently encounter inspectors who can get by in German, French, Polish, or Italian. But if a visitor's native language is Luganda or Urdu, and his English is too limited to explain his business in the U.S. to the inspector within 60 seconds, the inspector is going to send that traveler to secondary. Once in secondary (usually the INS gets stuck with such cases), the other inspectors can take the time to work with the visitor's English or find an interpreter.

By the way, interpreters are hard to get at land borders but easy to find at the kind of major international airports that have inspection stations. At an airport where I was stationed, we only needed to call the airline from Malaysia, Korea, India, or wherever to find an interpreter. Plan accordingly.

As much as pressures from fellow inspectors can keep inspections up to speed ("keep 'em movin'" seems to be the true—if unofficial—motto of the border), pressures from colleagues also keep inspectors from sending in a lot of secondaries. Just as inspectors don't want to work with slowpokes, they don't want to work with inspectors who lack the judgment to make decisions on the line. Some inspectors seem to send everybody to secondary. The following is not an uncommon scenario:

You've been sent to secondary. The primary inspector has also sent in a "secondary referral sheet" with notes on it about the reasons why he sent you in. The secondary inspector calls your name and glances at your secondary sheet. Then, before he even begins his inspection of you, he mutters to himself, "Why does that fool keep sending me this garbage?"

In a case like that, you can be sure that you're in for a short secondary. You'll soon be "down the road." Inspectors stuck with "garbage secondaries" will go to the primary inspector and chew him out for sending in such stuff.

Rules for Secondary

In Chapter 8, you'll learn a lot of specific, in-depth information about the questions inspectors ask during secondaries, as well as some tips on how to answer those questions so as to pass the border. But even from the beginning it will be helpful to keep in mind three basic rules for worry-free secondaries.

First, KNOW WHEN TO EXPECT IT. Do you have paperwork to fill out, either for Customs or Immigration? Are you importing things into the U.S., especially goods such as tobacco, alcohol, or (legal) firearms? Have you been denied admission to the United States in the past? Have you frequently been sent to secondary before, only to be admitted to the U.S.? Is there anything unusual about your appearance, vehicle, or reason for travel? In all such cases, you can expect to end up in secondary. So be a good Scout and be prepared. For more information, pay particular attention to Chapters 8 and 9.

Second, HAVE THE RIGHT DOCUMENTS READY. Are you entering the U.S. in order to work, go to school, or get married? Are you from a country that requires visitor's visas for the U.S.? In such cases, you'd better have the correct visa. Do you need proof of citizenship? Do you have the documents to prove citizenship? If you're an alien resident of the U.S., do you have your green card? Problems with documents lead straight to secondary. See Chapter 10.

Third, KNOW WHAT QUESTIONS TO EXPECT. Of course, each case is different, and so each inspection is different. But individual cases tend to fall into common categories. And so, inspectors tend to rely on the same questions over and over. See Chapter 8 for some of those.

"DUMPS" AND SEIZURES

As much as the ubiquity and growing powers of government bureaucracies may make America in the 1990s appear to be a police state (at least in comparison to the United States as envisioned by the Founding Fathers in the 1780s), you really don't have much to fear when crossing the border. Those who violate the law—or sometimes just piss-off the person in uniform—when crossing the border into dozens of countries across the globe are liable to be beaten, shot, arrested . . . or just disappear.

When crossing into the U.S., about the worst that is going to happen to you—provided you're not wanted and don't pick any fights—is that you'll be sent back to your country and/or have some of your goods (especially your car) seized by the government.

That knowledge may not make you very happy when your vacation plans have just been ruined and your new car is waiting for cheap resale in some government lot. But try to keep things in perspective, no matter what happens.

When an inspector turns you away at the border, he'll refer to it in his paperwork as "denial of admission to the United States pursuant to section such-and-such of the Immigration and Nationality Act." But when he talks among his fellow inspectors, he'll say, "I dumped him." To "dump" is inspector's parlance for the denial of admission to the United States. The verb has the correlative noun "a dump" for a person denied admission. If you're waiting in secondary, you may overhear inspectors talking among themselves, saying things like, "Is he a dump?" "Are you gonna dump him?"—all clearly in reference to you.

I've had experiences where a traveler, hearing himself spoken of in such terms, took offense and complained. All he succeeded in doing was making the inspector angry and lessening his chances of beating the border. Of course, no one likes to be called "a dump." But inspectors use such terms automatically, as jargon of the trade, just as police officers refers to "perps" and carnies to "marks." So never take a dump personally.

Most dumps and most seizures are avoidable. People are unaware that they require a certain visa, or proof of citizenship, or evidence of employment and residence in order to cross the border. Similarly, they may be unaware that they aren't allowed to bring oranges into the U.S., or ivory, or that if they persist in trying to cross the border after being dumped, they'll have their car seized.

Therefore, most dumps and seizures are due to ignorance.

And why wouldn't an average person—or even an extraordinary one—be ignorant of the complicated, convoluted, and sometimes just plain senseless laws and regulations that govern the United States border? I know that I was just as ignorant of border rules as anyone else until I started working for the INS, even though I had grown up in a town not more than 15 miles from the line.

But through the use of the information in this book, you can overcome the regulations. Learn the rules—written and unwritten—of the border, and keep in mind the tips I'll give in the chapters ahead. You'll learn to glide through inspections, avoiding dumps and seizures. In short, you'll be able to *beat the border*.

2

GUARDING THE BORDER

It's Not an Adventure, It's a Job

"What abhorrence can 'Nazism' inspire in young people when they are solemnly told that the frontier policeman who verifies a traveler's identity card is a Nazi?"

—Jean-Francois Revel
The Flight from Truth (1991)

I've been called a "Nazi," a "Fascist," and "worse than the Russians" by people trying to cross the U.S. border. You know what? None of those people got across.

I don't get mad, I get even. And so will every other inspector—if you give him reason to do it.

Inspectors on the U.S. border are not Nazis or Fascists or Bolshevik thugs. They're people, just people, with a job to do. They're doing that job as best and as fairly as they can so that they can pick up a paycheck every two weeks.

15

This chapter introduces you to the inside world of the border inspectors. It will give you an understanding of how inspectors ended up on the border, what they think about being there, and how they go about doing their jobs. Through an understanding of what kind of people the border inspectors are and what kind of job they have, you will be better prepared to beat the border.

TWO MISTAKES

There are two common notions about inspectors that are guaranteed to cause trouble for the traveler. First, a lot of people assume that inspectors are out to get them. Second, many people assume that border guards are stupid.

Let's first deal with the notion that inspectors are out to get you. It's almost a natural instinct for free men to enter into an encounter with authority (especially governmental authority, and even more so with any sort of police) as an adversary. From the school yard to the battlefield, it's Me vs. Him and Us vs. Them. In most cases, it makes sense to keep your guard up and do all the leading. But if you walk into an inspection with that attitude, chances are that it's going to backfire, and you'll end up in a fight you can't win. You'll end up being dumped, having your car seized, or maybe even getting arrested. The border will have beaten you.

Instead of walking into an inspection thinking that the inspector is out to get you, walk in with this fact in mind: inspectors are men (and women—the government, remember, proclaims itself "an equal opportunity employer") just like you.

If you've ever worked at a job you didn't particularly like (and who hasn't?), then you can start to appreciate what it's like to work for U.S. Customs or the Immigration Service. The work is like the Hobbesian state of nature: solitary, poor, nasty, brutish—but with long hours in place of short. The job is also occasionally dangerous and frequently dull.

AN INSPECTOR'S WORLD

When an inspector is in a booth, he's facing the world all

alone. Strangers appear one after another, and toward most of them he's indifferent. But an inspector will dislike more than a few. If he meets the rare person to whom he might take a genuine liking, that person will be gone in just a few seconds.

An inspector stands especially alone when occupying a booth at a land border. Every day he reads a new list of "lookouts," criminals who may be trying to cross the border, any one of whom could pull up and start shooting. Even though I carried a gun, I knew that it was mostly for show, to discourage potential trouble-makers. But if someone pulled into my booth and started shooting right away, I knew that I'd never draw my revolver in time to return fire. Anyone in law enforcement has the same kind of thoughts from time to time, but Immigration and Customs inspectors are special kinds of targets. They represent the U.S. government to anyone with a grudge against America. Inspectors are easy and accessible targets, as close as the nearest border.

During my years with the INS, there were always tips from time to time about such crazies. When Desert Storm was under way in Iraq, we were on constant alert for Iraqis or Muslim fanatics who might want to strike a blow for Saddam Hussein. Remember that if an inspector you meet seems a little jumpy or is very careful that you do not reach under the seat of your car or into your glove compartment. How does he know you're not going for a gun? Think of the inspector's situation, and relax.

So much for solitary and dangerous. How about poor?

Government jobs offer security and steady employment, but no one who's honest (that, of course, excludes congressmen, senators, and cabinet officers who turn lobbyist) gets rich off his government job. Inspectors start at GS-5 level pay (less than $16,000 a year when I was getting that salary). They advance, after several years, to the "journeyman" level of GS-9 (mid-to-high twenties). Not bad compared to what charwomen, cabdrivers, and cooks at McDonalds make, but by no means "Lifestyles of the Rich and Famous."

Nasty and brutish? Well, a few immigration and customs laws are probably unavoidable, and most are more or less tolerable, but many are silly, unfair, and useless. The inspectors who enforce those laws realize that fact as well as anyone. Nevertheless, they spend their days and nights on the line in order to make even the useless, unfair, and silly laws stick. Imagine how that wears on a person. One colleague described the work to me as "soul destroying."

I've already described the danger involved in guarding the border. So how about dull?

Being an inspector is usually about as exciting as working on the average assembly line. And it's just about as repetitious. In fact, doing inspections is very much like working on an assembly line, except the machine parts passing in front of you are people trying to get through the checkpoint. Time after time, day after day, you ask "What's your citizenship?" to everyone who passes in front of you. Even when you try to vary the questions, you still have to elicit the same basic information. Therefore, you always end up coming back to the same old questions.

Think about what would happen to your brain if you said "What's your citizenship?" 500 times a day. It gets to the point where inspectors ask the question in their sleep. Literally.

One inspector with whom I worked (and one of the best) fell asleep right after supper like everyone else who works shifts and overtime six days a week. Then she received a call from her mother, which woke her up. She picked up the phone, while still half asleep. Instead of saying "Hello," she said, "What's your citizenship?" That sort of thing happens to every inspector sooner or later.

How long are an inspector's hours? Unions have made the nine-to-five, 40-hour work week standard in the United States. But Customs and Immigration inspectors are government employees considered "essential personnel." They're forbidden by law to go on strike. As a result, their unions are strictly pro forma and powerless. The 40-hour week is just a dream on the border.

Inspectors work six days a week, usually including Sundays. Their one day off changes from week to week, so the usual enjoyment of the weekends—which most of us take for granted and which most of us look to like the Star of Bethlehem—is something an inspector sees only every two months.

All of the foregoing should give you some feel for the job an inspector has to do. To sum up, Customs and Immigration inspectors work long hours at a stressful job that is often stultifyingly dull and sometimes dangerous for low to middling pay. And, contrary to common prejudices, not all government employees loaf. Customs and Immigration inspectors work hard.

Now you know that inspections are no one's dream job. Kids think about growing up to be cops, but have you ever heard of the kid whose goal was to join U.S. Customs or the INS? None of that is designed to evoke your pity toward inspectors. But it does give you knowledge of their world. The old Indian proverb about not judging someone before you've walked a mile in his moccasins is a good one and as applicable to inspectors as to anyone else. You haven't worn the moccasins of an inspector, but you should know more about his job than the average person who approaches his first inspection full of false prejudices and misconceptions.

WORKING STIFFS

With the beginnings of some knowledge about the job, you're now prepared to cross the border without hassle—if you take the right steps.

The first step is to adopt this attitude: border inspectors are working stiffs, a lot like you. They're working stiffs with badges, guns, and the weight of the federal government behind them, but working stiffs nonetheless. They have jobs that they may or may not like, but it's mostly just a job to them. They're doing the best they can to do that job well and fairly and pick up a paycheck. Is that so different from most everyone else?

With such a view of inspectors, you're ready for the border armed with the right attitudes. You won't be angered by inspectors doing their jobs. And you won't be intimidated by them.

You won't be angered because you'll know why the inspector is asking you all those ostensibly intrusive questions and searching through your personal belongings. You'll know why he's ordering you around and perhaps treating you like a potentially dangerous criminal. It's all because he's doing a potentially dangerous job, and he doesn't know you from Adam. The inspector is only doing his job while taking sensible precautions to protect himself.

You won't be intimidated because you'll realize that behind the badge and gun and official attitude is a working stiff not unlike yourself. The inspector uses the tough-cop facade as a tool of his trade. No more, no less.

Guarding the border is, then, just a job. Most inspectors treat it as that, and nothing more. Of course, there are exceptions. Just as there are asshole cabbies, salesmen, accountants, and factory workers, there are asshole inspectors.

Every job has its assholes. Inspections has its share. I know because I worked with more than my share of them. But I didn't like them, and I never wanted to work with them ("John Asshole's on the early shift? Anybody want to trade shifts? Anybody?"). Inspectors stick together, but they also recognize the incompetents, slackers, and bullies among their own ranks. Inspectors rarely indicate that in front of what we always called "the traveling public." In private, however, inspectors will chew out the bad inspectors to their faces—and to the supervisors, if necessary.

Everyone can have a bad day. On the line, bad days and bad inspections are something with which even the smartest and most dedicated inspectors inevitably develop a personal acquaintance. I know that I (a natural hothead) tore into aliens when I shouldn't have because of times I took personally someone's attitude or remarks. But quickly I learned that there were better and smarter ways to behave. As a wise colleague advised me, "Don't get into a pissing match with 'em, just dump 'em." In short, I learned to distance myself from the inspections. I learned to treat the job as just a job.

BAD INSPECTORS: PETER, PAUL, AND MARY

Some inspectors never learn how to deal with the job. They are the bad inspectors—bad for the image of the United States, bad for their fellow inspectors to work with, and bad for you if you have the misfortune to encounter them at the border.

In my experience, every port of any size has three types of inspectors who cause problems for everyone. I'll call these types Peter, Paul, and Mary.

Peter is THE INSPECTOR WITHOUT COMMON SENSE. The one quality most important in making a good (or even competent) inspector is common sense. As you may already know, common sense is something difficult to measure by means of tests, interviews, and the rest of the usual apparatus used when considering someone for employment. That, I suppose, is the reason why both U.S. Customs and the INS seem to hire so many Peters.

Let me give you some genuine examples of the lack of common sense shown by the Peters with whom I've worked. Peter sends a 79-year-old woman to INS secondary because she's overstayed her visitor's visa for one week. Peter sends a diabetic, who identifies himself as a diabetic, to Customs secondary because he's carrying syringes and a bottle of insulin; the note to the secondary inspector reads "carrying drugs." Peter asks an Orthodox Jew why he's "wearing that cowboy hat."

Paul is THE POWER MAD INSPECTOR. The sad fact is that if you give a badge, uniform, and gun to some people, they immediately turn into tyrants. The sadder fact is that both the INS and U.S. Customs Service seem to attract more than their share of such people. My guess is that's because both agencies need to hire a lot of people every year. To fill the positions, both services end up with some of the tough-guy wannabes who couldn't make it in the armed forces, the Secret Service, or the FBI. Every inspector goes through a power-mad phase before he's got his legs under him in the new job. But the other inspectors with whom he works usually break him of that attitude pretty quickly. The ones who never learn are therefore, rare. Still, watch out for power-mad Pauls, because they *are* out to get you.

I've been unfortunate enough to work with Pauls at two different ports. Both Pauls were inadequate mentally, morally, and physically. They tried to make up for their shortcomings by treating honest travelers like misbehaving dogs.

One Paul was an Immigration Inspector who stood about five feet four. He liked to egg on tourists with hostile questions such as "Why should I let you go to the United States?" and "Is this really your wife?" This Paul was also very slow because he asked a lot of unnecessary questions of everyone (just another reason why no inspector liked to work with him). It's hard to fire civil service employees, but this Paul lasted only about a year with the Service. The second Paul was a Customs Inspector not much taller than the first Paul I described. The Customs Paul always wore black leather gloves and mirrored shades and carried an 18-shot 9mm semiautomatic pistol when everyone else on the line carried standard 6-shot Ruger revolvers.

In front of the booths at that port were yellow lines. The car waiting to be inspected was supposed to stay behind the yellow line, but people frequently drove across the line, almost always inadvertently. Most inspectors didn't get upset over line-crossers; they just explained to the driver that crowding the booths interfered with inspections and warned him not to do it in the future.

Customs Paul, however, wearing his Captain Law Enforcement outfit on his scrawny body, would scream and threaten the driver. Often, Customs Paul would make the driver back up and try again—sometimes several times. Then he would send everyone in the car to both Customs and Immigration secondary. The last time I drove through that port, Customs Paul was still on duty. Like I said, civil service employees can be hard to fire.

Mary is THE INSECURE WOMAN INSPECTOR. Mary has to prove that she's "as tough as a man." Don't get me wrong: I'm no misogynist. The fact is that most of the female inspectors with whom I've worked were fully as competent and qualified as the men (if not more so). But it's also a fact that a few women who work at traditionally masculine jobs that involve exercising authority feel the need to prove themselves over and over. They work strictly by the book, enforce every jot and tittle of the law (which they invariably know better than the men), and will never give a sucker an even break.

Whereas most inspectors, male and female, look upon their jobs as just jobs, Marys look upon the enforcement of the Customs and Immigration laws as a Crusade—and God help the infidel who violates those laws in even the smallest way. Marys get more dumps and more seizures than anyone else. They're star inspectors, but no fun to work with. It's even less fun to be on the receiving end of one of Mary's inspections.

One Mary with whom I worked was variously known as "the Dragon," "the Beast of the Apocalypse," and "Queen Bitch." And that was among fellow inspectors. Dumps used to stagger out of her secondaries looking as if they'd just gone 10 rounds with the middleweight champ.

The absolute worst mistake you can make is to treat a Mary dismissively, or "like just a girl." Never call Mary a "girl." Never try to intimidate her. You may as well try to intimidate a rock.

The best thing you can do at the border is try to avoid Marys. The problem is that there's no certain and easy way to identify a Mary until you're already trapped in the inspection booth with her. One tip: if you see a slatternly looking inspector whose uniform looks as sloppy as some of those on her male colleagues, you can be sure she's not a Mary. Marys invariably look like drum majorettes with guns. If you see two open booths, one with a man and one with a woman, go to the man. Thereby you'll avoid Mary. She *is* out to get you.

Despite all my warnings about the bad types of inspectors, you can rest assured that they are few and far between. Altogether, Peter, Paul, and Mary won't make up more than 10 percent of any inspection line. They may not be on the line at all. So keep in mind that when you're being inspected at the border, the inspector to whom you're talking isn't likely to be out to get you. He's just doing his job.

NOT STUPIDS

There's a second notion about inspectors that's just as common as the notion that inspectors are out to get you. It can be even more damaging to your chances of crossing the border quickly and easily—or even to your chances of crossing the border at all. The notion is that Customs and Immigration inspectors are stupid. If you think that, you couldn't be more wrong.

You may be surprised to discover just how well-educated inspectors are. The majority have college degrees. A large number have master's degrees. U.S. Customs seems to hire primarily as a career service—i.e., Customs Inspectors expect to work their whole careers with U.S. Customs or some other agency within the Department of the Treasury. The INS is more open to dilettantes. That's why so many Immigration Inspectors have college degrees.

There are two reasons for the presence people with of good educations in the INS. First, many Immigration Inspectors are schoolteachers. The INS employs such part-time inspectors who work for the Service as a second job at night (you'll find a lot of teacher/ inspectors on duty during second and third shifts, on weekends, or during summer vacations). So if you meet an inspector who treats you in the same way as did your tough geometry teacher in 10th grade, it's a fair bet that you're being inspected by a part-timer who is in fact a teacher.

Never believe that because he's a part-time inspector, however, that you will therefore have an easier time deceiving him. The schoolteacher/inspectors I knew were frequently tougher and shrewder than the full-time inspectors with whom I worked. Think of the teacher who gave you nightmares in high school. Now give that person a gun, a badge, and the authority of the U.S. Department of Justice. And remember to mind your manners when crossing the border.

The other reason you're likely to encounter smart and well-educated people in INS uniforms is something called the Outstanding Scholar Program. Through this, the Service hires recent college graduates who have high grades. The accountants and engineers with high GPAs go on to good jobs in the private sector, so the Immigration Service recruits tend to be sharp liberal arts grads who studied subjects like Schopenhauer's philosophy or Pound's *Cantos*. In short, such recruits are smart but unemployable—except in government service.

In any case, all inspectors receive training that makes them skilled in the ways of catching people who try to cross the border illegally (especially those who begin by thinking that they're smarter than those police on the line). The training takes place at the Federal Law Enforcement Training Center (FLETC) in Georgia. Inspectors' training is second in difficulty, intensity, and length only to the training of FBI special agents. In addition to roadwork, calisthenics, and general police training (target practice, hand-to-hand fighting, arrest and search techniques), inspectors master a year's worth of college-level Spanish and a law school's worth of immigration law.

PEOPLE SMARTS

If all of the above hasn't been enough to convince you that inspectors aren't the dummies you may have supposed, let me provide you with another piece of evidence.

Inspectors, by the very nature of their job, become "people smart" very quickly.

What do I mean by "people smart"? I mean that inspectors become experts in practical psychology. They turn into masters of reading people. The chief people-smart skill an inspector develops is the ability to tell when someone is lying.

An inspector's ability to spot a liar becomes a kind of instinct, or sixth sense. He may not always be able to fully analyze or explain why he knows someone is lying, but the inspector knows it nonetheless. He knows with a certainty that's inexplicable but real. An alien says A to the inspector, and the inspector knows—really knows—that the alien is lying. The truth may be B, C, or D, but, the inspector knows, it's definitely not A. So he sends the alien to secondary, where other inspectors work and work until they break him.

They're willing to work so hard because they know that when an inspector's instincts tell him an alien is lying, those instincts are inevitably correct. All inspectors develop the same instincts. If there's one genuine skill I've retained from my days on the line, it's the ability to spot a lie.

If you suspect that the people-smart skill of detecting a lie is an exaggeration on my part, let me assure you that it isn't. If anything, I've understated.

It's not so hard to understand how inspectors develop the skill if you think of it as analogous to the kind of skill anyone who works in a specific trade or job develops. Such skills always seem magical to the layman. A good and experienced auto mechanic can often diagnose what's wrong with a car just by listening to the engine run. A tailor can tell your sizes just by looking at you. A podiatrist can tell what sports you play just by watching the way you walk. And so on, with any number of other jobs, skills, and professions.

Why is that so? Because whatever it is the expert does, he does it over and over until it becomes automatic, a part of himself, an instinct and a sixth sense.

Now think about an inspector's job. He talks to hundreds of people, six days a week, week after week. Lots of people try to lie to him. He catches some and misses others. By trial-and-error, the inspector learns to spot a liar by the way the liar's eyes look, the way his hands move, the way his voice sounds. Soon, the inspector is catching more and more aliens who try to lie to him. Before long, the inspector is catching almost all the liars.

Why? Because the inspector's trial-and-error training is incredibly compressed. An inspector talks to more liars in a month than the layman does in a lifetime. How good at spotting liars do you think that inspector is going to be in a year? Or five? Or ten?

I've worked with inspectors who'd been on the job for 20 years. They could detect a lie or spot a dump, *without fail*, in the first five seconds of an inspection.

Moral of the story: inspectors are not stupid. Don't fool yourself with the expectation that they are. If you walk into an inspection with the wrong attitude, chances are that the border will beat you.

CUSTOMS VS. IMMIGRATION

What's the Difference?

When most people who aren't experienced border-crossers get inspected, they usually classify the experience as "getting through customs." Indeed, they usually think anyone at the border in uniform is "with customs."

As you know, I worked for the Immigration and Naturalization Service. One of the earliest lessons I picked up on the line is that calling anyone you meet at the border a "customs official" is a sure way to get off on the wrong foot with Immigration Inspectors. It's a common mistake and one that a little information can help you overcome.

This chapter explains the various officers whom you're liable to encounter at the border, how to tell them apart, and what their concerns are. Most often you'll deal with inspectors from one of two agencies: U.S. Customs and the INS. However, officers of other agencies also have the power to inspect on the border.

Let's look at the various kinds of border inspectors one at a time.

IMMIGRATION INSPECTORS

Immigration Inspectors are the uniformed officers of the Immigration and Naturalization Service (INS). Think about that name for a moment and you'll begin to understand the split personality of the INS. On the one hand, the job of the INS (or "the mission of the Service" as the manuals express it) is law enforcement, specifically the enforcement of the immigration laws. In its law enforcement capacity, the INS does the following: checks the documents of all persons arriving at every American port of entry; refuses entry (i.e., dumps) to those inadmissible under the law; watches to prevent the smuggling of aliens; and deports those persons in the U.S. illegally. On the other hand, the INS deals with naturalization, or aiding people with applications, petitions, and preparation for U.S. citizenship. Tough-minded law enforcement and help with naturalization don't always mix well.

Fortunately for Immigration Inspectors, they deal only with the first part of the "mission": law enforcement. The INS is under the control of the Department of Justice, along with such agencies as the FBI, the U.S. Marshals, and the Bureau of Prisons. The ultimate boss of the INS, then, is the Attorney General, although the Service itself is headed by a Commissioner of Immigration (an appointed office and therefore usually someone who knows nothing about the border but who contributed a lot of money to the winning presidential campaign).

A rule for you to keep in mind about Immigration Inspectors is that they enforce laws which deal with *people*. Therefore, it is under the immigration law that you can be denied admission to the United States.

Immigration Inspectors are the Rodney Dangerfields of federal law enforcement. They get no respect. There is no glamour associated with being an Immigration Inspector as there is with being an FBI special agent, for instance. Immigration Inspectors never chased Jimmy Cagney in the movies. The INS is also a latecomer to the border (Customs has been around since 1789, but the INS only since 1891), and its split personality has made it a kind of orphan in the government. The Service is always understaffed and always underfunded. Indeed, Immigration Inspectors have often not been treated like police at all. Until 1940, the INS was part of the Department of Commerce. Even today, Immigration Inspectors, despite guns and badges, are not classed as peace officers, lack full police powers, and have their authority strictly limited to the border.

The general public neither knows nor cares about the INS. People expect Customs inspection when crossing the border but often aren't sure what the Immigration Service is doing there. Many times, someone appeared in my booth, saw the patch on my arm that read "U.S. Immigration Inspector," and said, "Do I have to talk to you? I'm not immigrating."

Because of that lack of respect, Immigration Inspectors are notoriously suspicious and clannish (and not a little self-pitying). Immigration Inspectors refer to themselves as "IIs"—that is, "aye-aye," like the naval affirmative. Thus, I sometimes thought of a twist on the old Willie Nelson song, which became "Mamas, Don't Let Your Babies Grow Up to Be IIs." Like the cowboys in the song, IIs often feel "sad and alone, and a long way from home."

The very nature of the job, of course, makes IIs suspicious people. They have to be suspicious on the line. The habit of suspicion, however, has a tendency to carry over into private life. IIs spend many hours together day after day, week after week, facing an often indifferent and sometimes hostile public. After a while, it seems that the only person an II can trust is another II. At one port where I worked, the clannishness among IIs went to such lengths that the inspectors dated among themselves, married among themselves, baby-sat each other's children, and went only to each other's parties.

Something that few laymen realize is that the clannishness of IIs excludes Customs Inspectors. There's a constant rivalry between the Immigration Service and U.S. Customs. Customs is the senior service and therefore considers itself superior. The INS has the tougher job—at least in the opinion of IIs. Indeed, many more secondaries *do* go to the INS, both because of the great amounts of paperwork the INS requires and because it is ultimately under the immigration laws that aliens are dumped.

Usually the rivalry is friendly. Just as often, the rivalry is remarkably petty (remember that you're dealing with bureaucrats!). For instance, when the Customs office at one port where I worked got a new drinking fountain, the INS Port Director had to get a cooler for "Mountain Spring Water" for his office.

Sometimes, the Customs vs. Immigration rivalry goes far enough so as to interfere with the security of the border. In cases like that, Customs ignores the secondaries that IIs on the line send in, and Immigration resents the secondaries that Customs Inspectors send in. Then, the rivalry may be a boon to the potential border-crosser. But it's nothing to count on.

THE BORDER PATROL

Think of the Border Patrol as the Marines of the INS. They are the enforcement division, with full police powers. They call themselves "The Mean Green" because of their green uniforms—but also because they're tough, well-armed, and very enforcement-minded.

Since this is not a book about how to cross the border at unprotected spots (the spots which the Border Patrol is charged with protecting), I'm not going to tell you a lot about the Border Patrol, even though it's an interesting topic.

Although officers of the Border Patrol are called Patrol Inspectors, their job is not to do inspections like IIs. Rather, their mission is to protect the border at the open spaces away from lawful points of entry. Considering the fact that there are only a few thousand Patrol Inspectors for the tens of thousands of miles of the U.S. border, north and south, you can appreciate that the Border Patrol has an impossible job. Perhaps you can also understand why the U.S. has difficulties with illegal immigration.

But don't be fooled into thinking that Patrol Inspectors are bumblers. Where the politicians have the will—and the Border Patrol therefore has the resources—the U.S. border is *impassable* for illegals. Individual Patrol Inspectors are very capable.

The roots of the first Patrol Inspectors were in the Old West gunfighter tradition. One famous officer of the Border Patrol, Bill Jordan, literally wrote the book on gunfighting (*No Second Place Winner*). The Border Patrol still contains the best combat shots with a handgun of any agency (including the FBI) in federal law enforcement—and maybe the best shots in the world. When Delta Force needed training in how to handle handguns in close-quarters combat, it went to the Border Patrol for advice.

There are a few places where you're liable to encounter Patrol Inspectors in an inspectional situation—spots on the highways in south Texas, Arizona, and such places. These stations can be pretty far from the border and tend to be in rugged, isolated, rural areas. The Border Patrol uses such inspection stations to catch aliens who have entered the U.S. illegally and are heading for civilization via the highway. If you run into such Border Patrol stations, you'll see a sign telling you to stop for inspection, with pylons blocking the highway.

Do not try to run the blockade! Stop and talk to the Patrol Inspectors, who will ask you your citizenship and the same questions an II would ask at a lawful point of entry. Treat it just like any other inspection. Since the Patrol Inspectors are usually looking for illegal immigrants from Mexico, they may just wave you through if you don't "look Mexican."

CUSTOMS INSPECTORS

"The so-called taxes or duties, which the government levies upon imports, are a practical violation both of men's natural right to property, and of their natural right to make their own contracts."
—Lysander Spooner
"A Letter to Grover Cleveland" (1886)

Customs Inspectors are the other uniformed officers you'll see at every port of entry. They work for the U.S. Customs Service (USCS) and refer to themselves as "CIs" ("See Eyes"). The Customs Service is an agency within the Department of the Treasury. Just as the Attorney General is the ultimate boss for Immigration Inspectors, the Secretary of the Treasury is the top boss for CIs.

Since the Customs Service is part of Treasury, a big part of its job is collecting taxes on imports. Customs taxes are called duties, but they're taxes nonetheless. Everyone tries to avoid paying whatever taxes he can, so Customs Inspectors are always on the lookout for any sort of smuggling.

The Customs Service has been around since 1789—or since the United States became the United States under the American Constitution. If you have a tendency toward cynicism, you may note that the U.S. government made sure of its ability to collect taxes before it did anything else. Some distinguished characters have worked for U.S. Customs. Both Nathaniel Hawthorne and Herman Melville were CIs who used their government jobs to pay the bills while they wrote *The Scarlet Letter* and *Moby Dick*.

As such an old agency, and one that is usually well-funded and well-staffed (no doubt because it collects taxes), the Customs Service has a sense of security, almost a sense of superiority. U.S. Customs doesn't have a chip on its shoulder or feel the need to prove itself, as does the INS. Customs' secure attitude shows up in little things, such as the fact that CIs don't wear ties or bother with the spit-and-polish nonsense you see in the INS.

As someone being inspected, there are two things to keep in mind in regard to Customs Inspectors and Immigration Inspectors.

First, remember that Customs and Immigration are different agencies with different purposes and different laws to enforce.

Second, to understand the difference between Customs and Immigration, remember this rule: Immigration deals with people, Customs with goods. Put another way: Immigration deals with you, Customs with your things.

OTHER INSPECTORS

There are a number of officers with specialized duties whom you may encounter during inspection at the border. You're not

going to see them all the time, but just so that you won't be surprised when you do, I'll describe the officers and their duties.

Agriculture, Fish, and Wildlife Inspectors
These are inspectors under the control of the Department of Agriculture. They check to make sure that you're not importing diseased plants or livestock. You'll sometimes run into Agriculture, Fish, and Wildlife Inspectors, wearing their tan uniforms, helping CIs or IIs on the line. More often they're on the lookout for their special targets, especially at ports of entry through which enter a lot of produce and livestock. At a port on the Canadian border where I worked, an Agriculture Inspector would assist the regular inspectors about once a week in the summer.

U.S. Public Health Service Doctors
The U.S. Public Health Service (USPHS) is another old agency, founded in 1798 to prevent the spread of epidemics. Today, it's under the control of the Department of Health and Human Services. Public Health Service doctors are employed by the government, often because the government pays their medical school bills, then extracts several years' service in exchange. They wear uniforms that look somewhat like navy uniforms. Think of C. Everett Koop or Joycelyn Elders and you'll know how silly a doctor in uniform looks.

USPHS doctors are likely to be found at the Mexican border or inspecting arrivals from Third World countries, where diseases such as tuberculosis are still common. Doctors help determine if a person is lawfully excludable under the immigration law for health reasons.

The Coast Guard
The Coast Guard motto is *"Semper Paratus"* ("Always Prepared"), and as one of their duties, Coast Guardsmen are prepared to enforce customs and immigration laws at sea. You won't be inspected by the Coast Guard at regular ports of entry, but if you're inspected on board a ship, it will probably be by the Coast Guard. In such cases, the Guardsmen have the same authority and powers as IIs and CIs.

Customs vs. Immigration 39

DUAL INSPECTION

If both Customs and Immigration laws are in force at the border, then why aren't you inspected twice—once by U.S. Customs and once by the INS? Thirty years ago, that was just the system used at ports of entry. But there was comparatively little cross-border traffic in those days.

Nowadays, with multinational corporations, free trade agreements, and tourism as big business, there's a lot more travel across the United States' borders. Therefore, the government realized that the old, sensible, and secure system of two inspections by two separate agencies was too slow. The only place it is still used is at some airports and preflight sites.

At land borders and most other ports of entry, a system called "dual inspection" is used. Inspectors from one agency examine travelers for possible violations of both Customs and Immigration laws. Therefore, IIs act as CIs and vice versa. There's only one primary inspection.

Each agency (Customs and INS) cross-trains and authorizes officers of the other agency to act as one of its own. For example, I started work as an Immigration Inspector at a preflight port that did not use dual inspection. I was not empowered to enforce Customs laws, and, in fact, I really didn't know anything more about them than what I'd picked up in casual conversation with CIs. When I was transferred to work at a land border, I was not allowed on the line—even though I was an experienced inspector—until I had studied the Customs laws and had passed a written test on the subject. Then, I was on the line under the system of dual inspection, authorized to enforce both Immigration laws and Customs laws.

Nevertheless, I was still receiving the same pay that I had received when I was enforcing just the Immigration laws. Think about that fact for a moment and realize why I (along with most other CIs and IIs I've known) never liked dual inspection. In effect, I was getting paid once for doing two jobs.

Also, I realized that the dual inspection system reduced the effectiveness of both agencies and weakened the security of the border. The politicians who make the rules, however, like dual inspection. The system saves money for limos and Caribbean junkets. Remember dual inspection the next time you hear a politician lying about how "we must take control of our borders." If anyone in Washington were really serious about guarding the U.S. border, the first thing he'd do is eliminate dual inspection.

Dual inspection, however, can be good for you, the reader and traveler. Dual inspection works in favor of those who are eager to legally cross the U.S. border with a minimum of questions and fuss. It speeds up the traffic flow at border crossings.

Note, however, that dual inspection is used *only* for primary inspection. Since secondaries are more in-depth and involve details and fine points of the complex Customs and Immigration codes, secondary inspection is left to the specialists.

4
A LITTLE LAW

"... Congress has now gone on, for ninety years and more, filling great volumes with laws of their own device, which the people at large have never read, nor ever seen, nor ever will read or see; and of whose legal meanings it is morally impossible that they ever should know anything. ... Yet these laws, which Congress has not dared to require the people even to read, it has compelled them, at the point of a bayonet, to obey."

—Lysander Spooner
"A Letter to Thomas F. Bayard" (1882)

The average traveler doesn't need to know everything, or even a lot, about the laws that control the border. Hell, even longtime inspectors are continually surprised to find some law they've never seen before.

A basic background in the law, however, will better enable

you to beat the border. That's especially true in regard to the U.S. Immigration Code. Customs laws also govern the border, but compared to Immigration laws, they're pretty straightforward: you can bring in this, you can't bring in that. Immigration laws, on the other hand, are a maze. More importantly, the immigration laws are the ones that determine whether or not *you* cross the border.

Before we deal with details, there's a general rule to keep in mind about the immigration law: *there are differences between the laws as they are written and the way those laws are applied in the real world.* Inspectors find that they are frequently obliged to enforce a law when they are otherwise inclined to give a break to an alien. Conversely, inspectors can play dirty tricks on troublesome aliens, even when those tricks are contrary to the spirit—and even the letter—of the law. Watch out.

CAPSULE HISTORY OF IMMIGRATION LAW

The modern U.S. immigration laws are, as Mr. Spock might say, "highly illogical." Inspectors realize that problem. Worse yet, U.S. immigration laws are often unjust and just plain un-American.

Throughout most of the Republic's history, there were no federal restrictions on who entered the country, other than saboteurs and such. I can guarantee you that if my ancestors (who fled Europe as anarchists, draft-dodgers, and crooks) had to meet modern standards, I'd be writing a book on how to beat the border of Alsace, not of America. How about your ancestors?

From the 1880s to the 1920s, the United States Congress enacted its first restrictive immigration laws. In response to "the Yellow Peril," they started by excluding Chinese and Japanese. Then, prejudices against Catholics and Jews from Eastern and Southern Europe further reduced immigration. By the 1920s, immigration to the United States was pretty much limited to people from Northern Europe, and not even much of that was allowed. Historians agree that today's U.S. immigration laws have deep roots in ethnic and religious biases.

TODAY'S LAW

The fundamental law controlling the borders of the United States is the Immigration and Nationality Act of 1952. Among the pros, the law is often called the "INA," the "I&N Act," or simply "The Act." The INA has been amended four times—in 1965, 1976, 1986, and 1990—but, for the most part, the revisions have only served to make the law more complicated.

In addition to the Act, inspectors enforce other regulations which flow from it. Chief among those regulations are Codes of Federal Regulations (CFRs). CFRs are the dirtiest little secret of the federal government. Unlike other laws, the U.S. Congress does not make CFRs in public session. Rather, unelected bureaucrats write them, have them published in a monthly called *The Federal Register* (which no one other than bureaucrats reads), and, if the CFRs stand unchallenged for 90 days—as they always do—they have the force of law. If you think that's unconstitutional and un-American, then you're right. But that's the way the world works nowadays.

Inspectors also enforce Operating Instructions (OIs). An unelected bureaucrat also issues OIs, but in this case it's a very particular bureaucrat, the Commissioner of the INS. The Commissioner holds a sinecure and is appointed by the president. One doesn't have to know anything about the INA or have the slightest experience of guarding the border to be the Commissioner. As long as he's of the same party as the current president and has raised enough money for the campaign, he's in at the highest GS salary.

Most OIs are fully accessible to the public; you can find them in any complete law library. Some, however, are secret and will be known only to inspectors and other Service personnel. For example, the Commissioner might order IIs to stop and search all Iraqis, and only the insiders will know about it.

Finally, inspectors enforce interpretations, or court decisions about OIs. Since OIs can change quickly and arbitrarily, however, the federal courts often do not issue interpretations until after an inspector has interpreted the law, *as it affects you*, for himself. No

A Little Law

matter what form the law takes on the border, that law is always on the side of the inspector, not on the side of the traveler.

THE REAL WORLD

As law enforcement officers, inspectors know a lot about the law in their specialty, the border. But inspectors are neither lawyers nor judges. They don't make the laws or make a living from analyzing and writing about them. They only enforce them.

Inspectors have to apply laws that are often obscure or downright contradictory. They have to do the best they can on the spot. Inspectors work to interpret the law in practical situations under stress and in a hurry. Inspectors can—and do—make mistakes that lawyers argue about and courts overturn. Guarding the border is rarely an easy task.

THE 30-SECOND COURT

Think of each inspection as a 30-second court. The inspector has about half a minute to serve as a one-man judge, jury, and executioner. He determines in that short space of time whether you're going to get across the border, based on the INA, CFRs, and OIs as he interprets and applies them at the moment.

To get a favorable decision—i.e., to get across the border—in the 30-Second Court, you should use the information in this book to avoid the appearance of illegality and to make the inspector's job as easy as possible. Then he'll be more likely to apply the law in a way that will benefit you.

5

AUTHORITY OF BORDER GUARDS

Statutory, Implied, and the Real World

Under the law, the powers of Customs and Immigration inspectors are potentially very formidable. Also under the law, those powers are clearly defined, and, therefore, limited. In practice, inspectors almost always adhere strictly to those powers defined under the law. Almost always. The exceptions can make your trip a trial.

I'd like to claim that IIs and CIs stick strictly to the law because of principle—because, as the good government bullshit civics texts may have taught you in school, "our American system is a system of laws, not of men." But, of course, that would be a lie.

In the real world, the only world in which you'll have to worry about beating the border, inspectors stick to the law because it saves them trouble. Like every other bureaucracy, U.S. Customs and the Immigration Service operate on the time-honored principle of Cover Your Ass. During my years on the border, there were dozens of times when I wanted to pistol whip some loudmouth into silence. But I didn't do it, less because it would have been a gross violation of the law than because I would have lost my job and probably ended up in prison. Remember the Los Angeles cops who took a few whacks too many at Rodney King?

In real world situations, Customs and Immigration inspectors don't have to resort to violence in order to cause problems for the troublemakers. Even if an inspector cannot find a legal excuse to dump you, he can always delay your crossing. At airports, those delays can mean the difference between making a flight and missing one, which is the difference between making an important business trip or a long-awaited vacation and not making it. Every inspector on duty will be aware of that fact.

The basic rule to keep in mind with regard to the authority of inspectors, therefore, is this: in real world situations, an inspector can *always* make your crossing of the border difficult, if not impossible.

STATUTORY POWERS

Statutory powers of inspectors are those powers expressly stated in the law. Statutory powers are also duties for IIs and CIs. There is no way around them. They are the things that have to be done at the border.

As you can probably guess by now, the most basic statutory power of inspectors is the power to inspect. That's why *everyone* gets inspected.

If you want to swim across the Rio Grande along with a few hundred thousand Mexicans every year, be my guest. Otherwise, get inspected. I doubt that many Mexicans on the way to El Paso or San Diego are reading this book, anyway.

Even presidents get inspected. I've never been in on the inspection of a sitting president, but I did witness the inspection of an ex-president, when Ronald Reagan came through an airport where I was stationed. Reagan had been abroad, on a personal visit to one of his many rich friends. Weeks ahead of time, the Secret Service was in touch with the port. They double-checked the security clearances and backgrounds of the IIs chosen to do the inspection. On the appropriate day, the IIs put on their dress uniforms, shined their shoes, and went out to the private jet that Reagan was using. They verified that Ron and Nancy were indeed U.S. citizens. As the law required, everyone got inspected that day.

Another statutory power of inspectors is part of their power to inspect. Inspectors may, under the law, *interrogate you as much as is necessary.* Necessary, that is, in the inspector's opinion.

That power means that an inspector can, literally, ask you anything he deems necessary to determine whether or not you are excludable. It also means that you are obligated to answer him.

Don't get too worried, though. In practice, an inspector usually confines himself to the 30- to 60-second inspection. He also confines himself to asking the same basic questions, such as "What is your citizenship?" and "Where were you born?" But even in an ordinary inspection, an inspector often asks questions that would be rude and invasive in any other situation. For example, he may ask, "Are you married?" "Are you divorced?" "Is this woman your wife?" "What do you do for a living?" "How much money do you make?" "Have you ever been arrested?" Don't make the mistake of thinking that the inspector is asking you such questions because he really cares about your personal life (remember, inspections is just a job to him).

Also, don't make the mistake of thinking that the inspector is asking you such apparently invasive questions in order to piss you off. If he wants to piss you off, humiliate, and embarrass you, he'll ask you something like, "When were you last arrested for child molestation?"

Most of all, don't make the mistake of thinking that you don't have to answer the questions an inspector asks of you. In my experience, such an attitude is all too common among businessmen and lawyers. I can remember dozens of times when I asked lawyers and businessmen basic inspection questions, and the alien responded with something like, "Do I have to answer that?"

If he kept it a question, and I wasn't in my 10th hour on the line and, therefore, still feeling more or less human, I might patiently explain that yes, the law required him to answer my question.

More likely, I was in my usual bad mood, and I'd say, "You don't have to answer. But then again you don't have to cross the border. And you're not going to cross the border until you answer that question and any others I see fit to ask. Understand?" That usually convinced anyone that I was boss of the border, no matter how many keys to the executive washroom Mr. Businessman had or whatever law school class rings Mr. Attorney wore.

Sometimes, though, I'd encounter the self-important sort who would answer my questions with a statement instead of a question, by saying, "I'm not going to answer that." In such cases, I made sure he underwent a *thorough* secondary and missed his flight or business meeting. Even working stiff inspectors can be vindictive—if you give them a reason to be. So don't. And remember to answer an inspector's questions, as the law requires you to do.

If necessary, an inspector is also empowered to question you under oath. Such cases occur only in secondaries in which the inspector is going to dump you and you want to appeal to an immigration judge. It's not something you're likely to encounter.

Search and Seizure

As part of an inspection, Customs and Immigration inspectors are allowed by law to search you and *any* of your possessions. In most cases, during the typical 30- to 60-second primary inspection, an inspector will not look at any of your possessions (other than a glance at your car). But always keep in mind that the inspector maintains the authority to look through your things.

On the primary line, an inspector will frequently look in the trunk of your car. Don't worry about that; it's not necessarily a sign that the inspector suspects you're carrying contraband. Sometimes, an inspector will just decide to check the next car's trunk, no matter whether it's driven by a guy with tattoos and a ring through his nose or by a nun. He may decide that he'll inspect every 10th car, or every 27th. Little games like that help to beat the boredom of being on the line.

If you're sent to secondary, you can bet that not only will you have more questions to answer, but also that the secondary inspector will take a look through your goods. That's a certainty if it's a Customs secondary, and just about as likely if it's an Immigration secondary for any reason other than having documents stamped. Inspection of your possessions may range all the way to a strip search and the dismantling of your car. But don't be nervous, because ninety-nine times out of a hundred, secondary inspections of your goods are much less intrusive.

For example, if you're a man, an II will often search through your wallet. First, he'll ask you to remove the cash from it so that he can't be accused of stealing from you or of taking a bribe. Then, he'll look through the cards, receipts, slips of paper, photos, and other litter that invariably collects in a wallet. He may do this in front of you or he may do it out of sight. It's mostly a matter of personal preference. There are hundreds of possibilities for what the inspector will be looking for, things as varied as individual inspectors.

Some of the common reasons an inspector will search your wallet include:

- looking for credit cards, that, along with cash and traveler's checks, will show that you can support yourself during your stay in the U.S. without having to work illegally
- looking for business cards, pay receipts, and other evidence that indicates that the story you told about your business trip is a true one
- checking to see if you have a valid driver's license
- checking to see if you *don't* have a driver's license, library cards, bank cards, or other evidence of illegal residence in the U.S.

Similarly, an inspector will inspect a woman's purse. Purses are also good hideouts for small pistols, knives, Mace, or other weapons. At airports, inspectors will look at your carry-on bags. Frequently, they also contact the airlines to pull your checked bags so that those can be inspected.

You Can't Touch That

Keep in mind the fact that an inspector has the statutory power to search *any* of your possessions. One of the common mistakes of ignorance, and one that's guaranteed to cause you unnecessary trouble at the border, is to say to an inspector, "You can't touch that!"

I've heard that too many times to count, and, of course, any alien telling me how to do my job always made me at least a little bit angry. Every Customs and Immigration inspector thinks the same way.

Whenever someone said, "You can't touch that!" it was certain that I was going to touch that—because, of course, the laws of the United States granted me that power. Telling an inspector he cannot touch something of yours (wallet, purse, luggage, etc.) positively guarantees that the object is going to be inspected, and inspected with particular interest and thoroughness.

Why, then, do so many people persist in trying to tell inspectors what they can and cannot inspect? I think there are two reasons. First, people are ignorant of the laws governing the border, and they simply don't know that inspectors have the authority to search everyone crossing the border and any of their possessions. Second, people haven't adopted the attitude that inspectors are just working stiffs doing a job and who therefore have no personal interest in inspecting someone's possessions.

People try to avoid embarrassment over petty peccadilloes. Most of the time when a guy tried to tell me that I couldn't look in his wallet, it was because he had condoms there. He failed to realize that unless the object in question is illegal (prophylactics are not), the inspector isn't going to pay it much mind, no matter what his personal feelings. Inspectors maintain a certain measure of professional detachment—until you make the inspection personal.

No Warrants

Perhaps another reason why people make the mistake of thinking that an inspector cannot lawfully search them and any of their possessions is that they've watched too much TV. Cop shows always make a big deal out of search warrants. Someone who doesn't know much law gets fixed on the idea that all law enforcement officers require a warrant to search the car or luggage.

But, as you've no doubt come to realize by now, the border has its own rules. One of the basic rules of the border is this: *no warrants are required for an inspector to search you and any of your possessions.*

Isn't that a basic contradiction of the Fourth Amendment (which states, "The right of the people to be secure in their persons, houses, papers, and effects, against unreasonable searches and seizures, shall not be violated . . .")? Not on the border. An inspector can search *anything* of yours for *any* reason. Or for no reason at all. Unless you're driving an RV or sailing a houseboat across the border, your house is going to remain secure, but not your "person, papers, and effects." The simple fact is that Fourth Amendment protections against unreasonable search and seizure do not apply when you cross the border.

The legal reasoning by which the courts have decided that the Fourth Amendment does not apply (even to citizens of the United States) on the border is no more convincing than most other legal reasoning. But I'll give you the explanation. The courts have decided that because crossing the border is a voluntary action, basic Constitutional rights designed to protect people from the government are not in force there. There is also the practical reason for inspectors on the border having the power to search without a warrant: national security. Courts realize that we can't have people crossing the border while carrying guns, bombs, and maybe the odd nuke. So border inspectors must have the statutory authority to search for such things.

The lack of Fourth Amendment protections on the border is a dream come true for the kind of power-mad inspector I called "Paul" in an earlier chapter. Paul also suffers from the American disease of too much TV, so he's obsessed with "perps" who "get off on technicalities." Ever since his days of playing cops-and-robbers, Paul has dreamed of the powers that lie *in potentia* in the job of an inspector. At one port, I even knew a Paul who had left his job as a police officer for a job as an II, because, in his words, "Ya don't gotta bother wid Fourth Amendment bullshit." He's probably a supervisor by now.

Other Statutory Powers

As if the power to inspect without a warrant were not enough, inspectors have a host of other statutory powers that can keep you from crossing the border.

Inspectors can seize *anything* from *anyone* crossing the border as potential evidence. If you're carrying goods that might help prove that you're excludable from the United States, then an inspector can take it and keep it as evidence to put before an immigration judge.

Inspectors can arrest and detain anyone crossing the border (again, without warrant) if there is only suspicion of illegality. Like the power to inspect possessions without warrant, the power to arrest and detain is in part a matter of national security. Inspectors will, therefore, arrest and detain anyone suspected of being a terrorist or some other threat to the security of the United States. This is probably even more likely after the World Trade Center bombing and the assassination of those CIA employees in Langley, Virginia. It was a black eye to the already battered image of the INS when it was revealed that the World Trade Center bombers had slipped through inspections at JFK.

Inspectors have the power to board *and search* any vehicle. Of course, the inspector is going to look in your car if you drive it across the border. He's also likely to look in the trunk of your car. This power, however, applies more to searching your RV or boat. The custom exists that one asks permission before boarding a boat or ship ("Permission to come aboard, Captain?"). But if an II or CI inspects your boat, he'll be in charge ("I'm coming aboard to inspect the boat."). He can look anywhere and at anything on board.

I've had some lively experiences that arose from inspecting RVs. You'd be surprised at the number of RVs that cross the border: there are thousands, and at vacation time it sometimes seems that every fifth vehicle is an RV. Inspectors deal with RVs in different ways. Some just ask the driver to make everyone on board come up front so the inspector can ask the usual questions. Sometimes they'll send an RV down the road without boarding the vehicle or inspecting the inside. This sort of inspection is used especially with elderly travelers heading south on vacation. It's also used with families that look like the Cleavers.

It's a judgment call, but I made it a practice to always board an

RV and take at least a cursory look at the inside. Usually, I walked up and down the interior, opening doors to rooms (especially bathrooms, where illegals like to hide), and looking into cupboards, closets, or anyplace that I thought might be big enough to hide an alien. Once I glanced into the bedroom of an RV and saw a likely looking lump lying under a blanket on the bunk. Underneath was a woman of about 20 and she was completely naked. It turned out that she was a U.S. citizen and therefore good to go—but the driver, a married man in his 50s, had been too embarrassed to tell me about her. She wasn't his daughter, by the way.

The biggest problems I met when boarding and searching RVs came from dogs. One of the first times I opened the door of an RV, a dog jumped out on me and almost knocked me over (not to mention scared the shit out of me). Fortunately, it was a big, friendly Lab and meant no harm. Not long after that, a dog in the back of an RV lunged at that favorite target of ferocious canines, the family jewels. I blocked him with my knee, then slammed him on the snout with a flashlight. That caused the dog to back up into perfect range for a front snap kick, which I promptly delivered. The kick bowled over the dog.

The owner complained about my "unnecessary violence."

Another time, a ferocious German Shepherd made as if to bite me. I slammed the RV door in the dog's face and told the owner that I'd shoot the beast if he didn't tie it up. That prompted another complaint. From then on, before I boarded an RV, I always asked the driver if there were any dogs on board. If he said there were, I made sure that he had restrained the animal before I inspected the vehicle.

My procedures worked well and saved everyone (owner, dog, and especially me) lots of problems. Keep this advice in mind if you're ever crossing the border in an RV with a dog on board: restrain the animal and warn the inspector.

Car Seizures

The ultimate part of the search and seizure powers authorized to inspectors and commonly applied at the border is the power to seize vehicles. This usually applies to taking your car.

Think about that for a minute. For violations of the rules of the border, an inspector can take your car. Nowadays, most of us depend on our cars for getting to work and for our essential everyday living. Unless you own a house, your car is probably your biggest investment. But pleading all that to an inspector won't make a bit of difference to him. Taking cars is one of the best ways to advance in the Immigration Service.

Those who have their cars seized are always surprised to have it done. They shouldn't be. They should be expecting to have their cars seized.

The reason they shouldn't be surprised is that the law under which an inspector seizes a car is based on a conspiracy charge. Unless you're caught carrying drugs, in which case your car can be seized under the Customs regulations (it was called "Zero Tolerance" when I was an II, but I don't know that such a system is still in place now that a noninhaling pothead is in the White House), *your car will not be seized the first time you are refused admission to the U.S.* Rather, it will be seized the second time you are dumped. The seizure is based on the assumption that you know you were inadmissible to the U.S. because you'd already been dumped. Nevertheless, the INS assumes, you knowingly and willingly tried to cross the border illegally.

When an inspector dumps you, he'll explain to you that your car may be seized if you persist in trying to cross the border. Sometimes, if you're the kind who pisses off an II when he dumps you, the kind who he suspects will try to cross the border illegally, he won't advise you of the possibility of having your car seized. But he will write in his report that he advised you. Thereby he leaves a paper trail that allows him to seize your car the next time. You'll protest as much as you can that he never warned you, but the paper record of the INS will state otherwise. Your word against the word of an II and documentary evidence to back him up will be worth nothing. Beware.

The rule to keep in mind is: *do not persist in trying to cross the border once you've been dumped.*

Inspectors want to seize your car. That sentiment is not due to any personal animosity or desire to "get" you (although, to tell the truth, animosity does sometimes play a role), but to the way the system has been set up. The system awards promotions on the basis of how many cars an inspector seizes. In the eyes of the INS, a good inspector is one who seizes a lot of cars. The best inspector seizes the most.

The Burden of Proof

American law grew out of the English Common Law. That long tradition is a great boon to freedom because, unlike Roman law, the Napoleonic Code, and other traditions of law around the world, under the Common Law, you are innocent until proven guilty.

Innocent until proven guilty. That's a fundamental fact of life for every American, something we take for granted, a basic truth we all absorb almost from the cradle. If the government accuses you of a crime, it is up to the government to produce sufficient evidence to prove beyond a reasonable doubt that you are guilty of the crime because you are presumed innocent. Everyone knows that. In America, everyone is innocent until proven guilty.

Not on the border.

On the border, much of the world you know and take for granted is turned upside down. This fact is no clearer than in matters of presumed guilt and the burden of proof. On the border, not only the Constitutional guarantees of search and seizure are invalid but also the whole tradition of American law.

Therefore, on the border, you are guilty until proven innocent. On the border, the burden of proof is on you.

Those are two facts that can most affect your crossing of the border. Those are two rules governing all the other laws of the border. Those are the two bases of the powers that Immigration and Customs inspectors have over you.

The inversion of American traditions that is in place on the border gives inspectors potentially extraordinary powers over you—if they decide to exercise that power.

It behooves everyone who wants to beat the border to avoid even the appearance of illegality. The knowledge and techniques in this book will enable you to do that.

IMPLIED AUTHORITY: WEAPONS

Implied authorities of inspectors are those not expressly stated in the law. They are derived from court decisions and sometimes it seems made up from whole cloth. There's no need to get into the minutiae of implied authority available to inspectors. Most of it will have no practical effect on your ability to cross the border. But there is one aspect of implied authority that can have a great effect on you. That is the authority of inspectors to perform their duties armed.

The courts have decided that IIs and CIs, like other federal law enforcement officers, have the authority to bear arms. Not all inspectors, however, will carry weapons. I began my career with the INS, for example, at a preflight inspection port outside of the United States. As you may expect, foreign governments prefer that U.S. government officials not carry weapons while in their airports. So I didn't perform my inspections armed until I transferred to a land border in the U.S.

Inspectors with whom I worked at the airport and who started with the INS or Customs at the land borders didn't like to go about their duties unarmed, no matter where they worked. One II at the airport told me, "I feel naked without a gun on my hip." By the way, inspectors at airports inside the United States, such as JFK, will be armed.

A pistol used defensively, even when it's just in a holster on an inspector's hip, tends to discourage violence. That's the real reason why inspectors, like other law enforcement officers, carry guns. Shooting incidents at the border are exceedingly rare (not for the Border Patrol). Inspectors almost never draw their guns, much less fire them.

A weapon that is more likely to be used on the border is one many inspectors find more practical than a gun, and therefore they tend to prefer it to a firearm. That weapon is a flashlight (sometimes lead-weighted). A good flashlight is, in effect, a stronger, harder, and more efficient kind of billy club. Since a flashlight is a practical tool for inspections (being used, for example, to look in the backseats of cars), one likes to have a flashlight in the booth anyway. Also, a flashlight doesn't draw attention to itself, and most troublemakers are too stupid to expect a flashlight to be used as a weapon. A wise inspector can always have a flashlight in his hands, ready to strike a troublemaker the moment he reaches for a weapon. By then it's too late for the troublemaker, because one blow from the kind of flashlights IIs prefer will lay out anyone short of Andre the Giant.

When inspectors do carry guns, they carry pistols. IIs and CIs won't have the shotguns and submachine guns you sometimes see carried by the Border Patrol. There's simply no need for such weapons during inspections. When I was with the Service, we carried Ruger revolvers, .357 caliber, with short barrels. Even then, inspectors were switching over to 9mm Glocks, a switch that may have been accomplished by now.

THE REAL WORLD

This chapter began with a brief explanation of the differences among the powers of inspectors: statutory, implied, and the real world. Having already dealt with statutory and implied powers, it's now time to talk about the topic that has the most importance for you as you try to cross the border—the real world.

There's often a world of difference between the ideal world of the border, as it's spelled out in law and policy, and the real world of inspections. In some cases, that fact can work against your ability to cross the border speedily and without more than a minimum of bother. But in the case of the authority of inspectors, the real world works in your favor.

The real world of inspections favors you because, despite the Draconian powers inherent in the laws, real-world inspections are almost always strictly controlled, nonthreatening, and as quick as they can be.

Strictly controlled? Yes, because IIs and CIs on the line will try to work as much "by-the-book" as they can. This keeps them out of hot water with their supervisors, who don't have to deal with complaint letters, calls from congressmen, loud-mouthed lawyers, and the rest of the things bureaucrats detest.

Nonthreatening? Yes, because the inspector is just doing his job. He's asking you the same questions and telling you to do the same things that he tells hundreds of others to do every day. Even if his voice is loud and his manners stern, that's just a game face he puts on with his uniform.

As quick as they can be? Yes, because, you remember, an inspection is like a 30-Second Court. The inspector wants to get your inspection over as soon as he can so that he can get to the next inspection, keep the traffic moving, and go home when his shift is over.

EXCLUSIONS

How and Why

No one wants to be excluded from the United States. It's even worse to be "dumped"—as being excluded is called in inspector's parlance. Being dumped even sounds bad.

In order to avoid being dumped, it is helpful to know the reasons, legal and semilegal, why an inspector may exclude you from the United States. Just as important and just as helpful is the knowledge of what sort of questions and investigations inspectors use on their way to excluding someone from the United States.

GOOD DUMPS VS. BAD DUMPS

Recall Chapter 3, wherein you learned just how clannish inspectors can be. As part of that clannishness, inspectors talk about their dumps among themselves. Every inspector becomes a collector of dumps, hoarding tales of his own and those of his colleagues for the dead hours on the line when inspectors trade war stories. Inspectors constantly compare and talk about their dumps. They are proud of the good ones. They'll even collect bad ones in order to improve their performance and further their careers.

How does one tell good dumps from bad dumps? Surprisingly, the differences are pretty clear cut.

Good dumps begin with criminals. Every inspector is happy to keep a criminal out of the United States (we already have too many of the home-grown variety). Inspectors, remember, are law enforcement officers, and law enforcement officers are in the business of stopping, controlling, and protecting citizens from criminals. Dumps that involve criminals go from merely good to better when those criminals dumped are guilty of serious offenses or violent crimes, such as armed robbery, murder, or rape.

A special type of criminal is another first-rate dump: terrorists or other national security risks. Any inspector who catches a spy, a terrorist, or similar character can justly boast among his comrades. That's something every inspector craves. Such dumps aren't as rare as you might think, either. I've personally participated in cases involving a couple selling computer technology to the Soviets, a North Korean spying on rocket technology at NASA, and a gunrunner for the PLO.

More common good dumps are inspections that require in-depth investigation and interrogation, tricking, and "breaking" an alien who has been lying to the inspectors. Inspectors love to "break" liars by whatever means necessary—persistence, tricks, lies, threats. Trading tales of how inspectors break an alien is a favorite pastime among IIs and CIs. It goes on all the time. The practice serves as a kind of informal school of how to do an inspection. Even rookie inspectors rapidly build up a vast store of practical examples on which they may draw during their own inspections. Thereby they develop "people smarts."

Dumps that might otherwise be classified as bad dumps automatically become good dumps when an inspector dumps someone who causes trouble for the other inspectors. This is largely a matter of the clannishness of inspectors, the "us vs. them" attitude in which inspectors are "us" and everyone trying to cross the border is "them." When at work on the border, inspectors' first loyalties are always to other inspectors. Therefore, anyone, no matter how minor his offense, approaches in the eyes of an inspector the level of a criminal as soon as he starts to cause trouble for inspectors. Remember that fact whenever you're tempted to crack wise or otherwise cause problems when being inspected.

Bad dumps are much simpler. For the most part, they involve exclusions based on minor or purely technical offenses. Perhaps the most common sort of bad dump involves a recently expired visa, especially when the alien was not aware that the visa had expired. In most such cases, the alien gets a valid visa (or a waiver) and is across the border the next day.

STATISTICS

Mark Twain was right about a lot of things. With a kind of common sense that more and more seems absent in America, Twain remarked, "There are three kinds of lies: lies, damned lies, and statistics." As you may have guessed, then, the Immigration Service loves statistics.

Inspectors learn to hate statistics, because, for the most part, promotions are based on statistics. Especially important is the number of dumps an inspector accumulates. If our typical working-stiff inspector wants to move up a step on the civil service ladder so that he can pay for his kid's college tuition, buy a second car, or have the roof on his house repaired, he has to keep a certain number of people from crossing the border. There's no set number that he has to dump, but he knows that he has to keep up with the other inspectors around him. Therefore, every inspector has the incentive to make dumps, even the ordinary, working-stiff inspector who isn't otherwise out to get anyone. The gung-ho, career-minded inspector, with an eye on the supervisor's stripes, has even more incentive to make a lot of dumps—good, bad, and indifferent. He'll dump anyone he can, and some he can't.

Why do even bad dumps help an inspector's career? It's a mat-

ter of statistics. Statistics do not differentiate between good dumps and bad dumps. Statistics measure quantity, not quality. Statistics are just numbers, so by the criteria of statistics, keeping out a tourist whose visa is one day out of date is as important as keeping out a convicted rapist.

Perhaps now you can understand why many inspectors hate statistics. In the private exchange of war stories among themselves, IIs give their greatest respect to the inspectors who get the most good dumps. But in the bureaucratic system of the Service, an inspector who dumps a rapist, two armed robbers, and a cocaine courier is worth less than an inspector with 20 dumps for expired visas. The latter inspector is the one who'll make supervisor. Quantity, not quality, runs the Service. That's probably why the INS is as screwed up as it is,

Keep in mind that an inspector always has an incentive to keep you from crossing the border, because it helps his stats. Use the information in this book to do everything in your power to avoid giving an inspector an excuse to add you to his statistics.

THE OLD 33

From 1952, when the basis of all further immigration laws went into effect, until 1991, when the Immigration Act of 1990 ("ImmAct 90") started being enforced, the reasons for which an alien could be excluded from the United States were put into 33 categories. Even now, the exclusions are just a minor revision of those old 33 grounds for exclusion. But as congressmen, bureaucrats, and other lawmakers are prone to do, they wrote the 1990 ImmAct so that the old 33 grounds for exclusion (which were easily memorized and provided a handy code for IIs and CIs) were put into an awkward, hard-to-memorize and hard-to-talk-about group of five related sections and subsections.

New inspectors, however, still learn the old 33, and veteran inspectors know them well. Therefore, the old 33 provide a lingo still used among IIs. Inspectors assume that you don't know anything about the immigration law, and, therefore, within earshot of an alien, IIs will often refer to their suspicions in terms of the old

33. It behooves you, the reader, to familiarize yourself with those grounds for exclusion.

For example, if an II (or CI) on the line suspects that you are excludable because of a criminal record, he'll send you to secondary. The inspector on the line will never tell you outright exactly why you're being sent to secondary or exactly what he suspects you of. But if you're careful and observant, you may overhear the inspector say to the secondary officer something like, "I think he's a nine." Under the old 33, the ninth exclusion was for having a criminal record. And so, a "nine" is a suspected criminal.

The inspector thinks you won't know that, but now you do. With such foreknowledge of why you've been sent to secondary, you can conduct yourself during the secondary inspection so that your are not dumped. Knowledge is power. Use it to beat the border.

A complete list of the old 33 grounds for exclusion may be found in Appendix II. Many were rarely used. Some common ones to keep in mind, however, include:

- a "twelve" is a prostitute
- a "twenty-two" is a draft-dodger
- a "twenty-three" is grounds for exclusion based on any drug offense, from trafficking to possession

THE NEW CATEGORIES

If you read the papers, you know that Congress and other assorted elected criminals call, from time to time, for "reform" of the U.S. immigration laws. For the past 10 years or so, we've been in the midst of one of those "immigration crises," which politicians and newspaper pundits invent whenever votes and sales are sinking. The aspect of the most recent "crisis" that affects you trying to cross the border is the last "sweeping reform," the Immigration Act of 1990.

In fact, ImmAct 90 wasn't a "sweeping" reform—or much of a reform at all. For the most part, ImmAct 90 rearranged the old 33 grounds for exclusion into eight larger categories. Let's look at them one by one.

Health-Related Grounds for Exclusion

Ever heard of Typhoid Mary? Just one person infected with a communicable disease can spread sickness across the globe— unless stopped at the border. That is why health-related grounds for exclusion begin with communicable diseases.

But don't worry that if you have a cold or the flu, an inspector is going to turn you around at the border and tell you to come back when you're well. Exclusions for communicable diseases involve serious diseases, ones which the U.S. government considers life-threatening, a danger to public health, or the beginnings of a pandemic.

The list of diseases covered under this rubric is subject to change by the U.S. Public Health Service. Nowadays, the only diseases with which border guards are liable to be concerned are tuberculosis and AIDS. Either is grounds for exclusion— although the AIDS lobby has enough political and media pull to allow HIV-infected people to be admitted to the U.S. on a waiver for scientific conferences and similar gatherings.

How does an inspector tell if an alien has AIDS or tuberculosis? None too easily. Inspectors are not doctors, and doctors are really the only people qualified to make such diagnoses. Therefore, in the law books it states that USPHS doctors must make the determination if an alien is excluded because of a communicable disease.

Remember, however, that we're dealing with the real world, not the ideal world of law books. As always in the real world, if an inspector suspects that you're suffering from a communicable disease, he'll find a reason to dump you. How can he get away with that? Simply because of that catch-22 of the border: the burden of proof is on you. You don't have AIDS or tuberculosis? How can you prove it without medical tests and documents?

I've seen people dumped because, as it read on the secondary referral, "he looks like he has AIDS." I've seen others dumped because they had AZT (a drug used to treat AIDS) in their luggage. Of course, you can determine with some degree of certainty that a person has an advanced case of AIDS by the wasted and abnormally thin look, skin lesions, and other signs (did you see

Beat the Border

the movie *Philadelphia*?). Likewise, a bloody cough is an indicator of tuberculosis.

But again, CIs and IIs aren't doctors, and their diagnoses are based on guesswork and superficial observation. No one wants to get too close to someone he suspects might be carrying a communicable disease. Once I was on the line when an alien appeared for inspection, and he was obviously very sick: thin, coughing, and as yellow as a ripe banana because of jaundice. None of us would go near this alien to inspect him. We made him stand behind the red line in front of the inspection booths until we got a supervisor to do the inspection—from 10 feet away.

Don't think we were being overly cautious. I once caught a severe infection from handling the passport of an East Asian traveler, then unsuspectingly rubbing my eyes with germ-laden hands. Americans don't have immunities to lots of Third World diseases.

Mental disorders are another reason for exclusion on health-related grounds, and sometimes they're not as difficult to spot as communicable diseases. From my experience, the two chief giveaways of mental disorders are bizarre behavior and drugs. The latter include medicines for schizophrenia and other disorders, drugs that nowadays allow people with mental problems caused by chemical imbalances to lead more or less normal lives.

I worked at one port at which we were fortunate enough to employ a part-time II who had a master's degree in clinical psychology and whose day job was as a mental health counselor. He could identify all psychoactive medicines and tell the rest of us if they indicated an alien should be dumped. As long as the aliens were being treated and didn't seem dangerous, we usually let them travel.

Again, USPHS doctors are supposed to make the determination of mental disorders, but in the real world, inspectors do the job themselves. Maybe we were a little lenient with possible mental disorder dumps because we thought all of us were a little crazy from working on the border.

The tip-off of bizarre behavior could be more interesting. A case in point was an alien who appeared for inspection carrying a shoe box. The inspector asked the usual questions, then said, "What's in the box?"

"Can't see," came the reply.

Now, of course, the inspector was intrigued, and also determined to find out what was in the box. After all, it could have been a gun or a bomb. The inspector played along.

"Why can't I see?"

"It's for the president. Only he can see."

Knowing that threats to the president (even ones that might not appear serious) had to be reported to the Secret Service, the inspector asked, "Why does the president need to see it? It's not something to hurt him, is it?"

"No, but it's important. Vital, you might say, to the security of the free world."

"I see." By now the inspector had determined that the alien was harmless, if crazy. He brought him to secondary and, in the course of further inspection, found out that the guy had forgotten to take his medicine and had slipped away from his Canadian halfway house. The inspector called the director of the place to pick up the alien and gently dumped him—but not before he surrendered the shoe box to a supervisor, who promised to deliver the contents to the president "through all appropriate official channels."

The box contained a contraption made mostly of dry cells and aluminum foil, plus two pages of directions printed by a very precise hand. The device, the directions claimed, was "the solution to the energy crisis" and "the true key to cold fusion."

The final reason for exclusion on health-related grounds is drug addiction. There are telltale physical signs of drug addiction for which inspectors always watch. These include needle tracks and drug paraphernalia. Most of the drug dumps I encountered were Canadians using their socialized national health insurance to pay for stays at posh detox centers in the United States.

Crimes Involving Moral Turpitude

"What the hell does 'moral turpitude' mean?" shouted one alien after he was dumped.

You can consult your own dictionary, but I will let you know that "turpitude" comes from the Latin *turpis*, which means "base," "wicked," or "corrupt." I think you get the idea.

In fact, "crimes involving moral turpitude" is a phrase in legalese that stands for one of the most common reasons why an alien is excluded from the United States. Since it's such an awkward tongue twister, inspectors usually don't say "Crimes Involving Moral Turpitude." Instead, they say "CIMTs" ("See-Eye-Em-Teas"), and you'll often hear the term bandied about within earshot of aliens. If you're sent to secondary, for example, and the inspector says something like, "Check him for CIMTs," you'll know what's cooking.

Many different crimes count as CIMTs. A useful (but not foolproof!) general rule to keep in mind about whether a crime is a CIMT: felonies are CIMTs; misdemeanors are not. But remember, there are exceptions!

Some examples of crimes that qualify as CIMTs are armed robbery, arson, blackmail, burglary, counterfeiting, felony assault, kidnapping, manslaughter, murder, and rape.

As you can see, those are serious, hard-time crimes, not the sort of things that an unlucky person picks up on his record through youthful indiscretion. Dumps for CIMTs are dumps of real criminals, not exclusions for minor technical offenses. Any inspector will be more than happy to keep someone with CIMTs out of the U.S.

What are some of the "minor crimes" that don't count as CIMTs? Examples include carrying a concealed weapon, drunk and disorderly, gambling violations (usually), harassment, passing bad checks, traffic violations, and vagrancy. You may readily see how those crimes are relatively minor matters for which anyone might be picked up. More than a few of my colleagues in the Immigration Service had their teenage D&D arrests on their records, and those weren't enough to disqualify them from being hired by the Department of Justice.

Sometimes, however, even hard-core criminals have nothing but non-CIMT crimes on their records. I once inspected a German Hell's Angel (yes, Virginia, there are such rough beasts!) who I

sent to secondary, expecting an easy dump. The *Motorradfahrer* wouldn't admit to anything, so we got his record from Interpol (all in German, which, fortunately, I read). He had a number of minor arrests and a conviction for *Verbotenwaffenhandlung* (literally, "handling forbidden weapons"), which didn't seem to qualify as a CIMT.

I couldn't seem to find a legal reason to dump the Hell's Angel, but I also wasn't about to let him into the U.S. So I just made him sit while I pretended to work on his case. After a few hours, he grew sufficiently pissed-off that he decided he didn't want to enter the U.S. after all. That was good enough for me.

As always in the real world of the border, when an inspector is really determined to keep you out of the country, he'll find a way to do it. Or invent one.

CONVICTION VS. ADMISSION

The job of a border inspector is made all the easier because of another peculiarity of the immigration law. Under the I&N Act, an inspector does not need proof that an alien has been convicted of a crime in order to exclude that alien from the U.S. Rather, the inspector needs only the alien's admission of such a conviction— or even of just an arrest.

Clever inspectors, always eager to add more dumps to their statistics, will use every trick they can think of to get an alien suspected of a CIMT to admit to arrests or convictions. Inspectors call this "breaking" a suspect, and good inspectors can be very tricky in getting someone to admit to a crime.

One of my favorite tricks is a common one used by IIs. It was taught to me during my first weeks on the job by a 15-year veteran of the Immigration Service who had used the trick to dump hundreds of aliens.

I would pretend to be a friend to the alien when, in fact, all I was looking for was an excuse to dump him. I'd say, "We have reason to suspect that you have a criminal record, and I don't want you to lie to me about it. That'll just make things harder for you. Now, I can look up your whole record, but that will take time. So I want you to be honest, make things easier for both of us, and just tell me what you've been arrested for. Those may or may not be grounds, under the U.S. immigration law, for you to be kept from crossing the border." Then, once I'd established myself as a no-nonsense kind of guy who was willing to give an alien a break and play fair, I'd spring the trap: "For example, you don't have to worry about arrests for things like traffic violations, drunk and disorderlies, or burglary."

Notice that I mentioned two non-CIMTs (not grounds for exclusion) along with one (burglary), which is a CIMT.

That simple tactic was very effective in getting responses such as, "Oh yeah, I did have that one arrest for burglary." And then I had my dump. What did I care if an alien pleaded that he'd been tricked? I'd obtained that crucial admission of guilt, which allowed me to exclude him from the U.S.

Inspectors use dozens of other traps to obtain admissions of CIMTs. Oftentimes, inspectors have on hand the records to prove arrests and will just practice their breaking tricks in order to keep the boredom of the job from becoming overwhelming. You can catch the general flavor of such tricks from the example I've given.

There are two lessons to learn from my example. First, a CI or II is not your friend, no matter how much of a "good cop" he may pretend to be. He may be just a guy doing a job, but that job is to keep you out of the U.S. Second, if you do have a record of CIMTs, it's better to stay on the outside of the border and apply for a waiver before you try to enter the U.S.—unless you're an expert liar with an unbreakable story.

CRIMINAL EXCLUSIONS OTHER THAN CIMTs

There are a few crimes that do not qualify as CIMTs but can nevertheless get you dumped under the category of "Criminal and Related Grounds." These crimes involve what is commonly called "vice," specifically, gambling and prostitution.

Prostitutes are often called "twelves" by IIs because under the old 33 exclusions, 212(a)12 was the section of the INA that excluded prostitutes. Women (or men! It happens.) convicted of

prostitution will be dumped at the border, as will pimps (or "procurers" as the INA phrases it).

At some border crossings there are lots of dumps of "twelves," because the girls on the lax side of the border think that they can make more money on the American side. They're usually right. You probably wouldn't be surprised to hear that a lot of Mexican working girls want to get across the border, but it might be news to read that there are also many Canadian whores who work both sides. Despite its reputation as a scrupulously law-abiding country, Canada tends to have relaxed laws (and even more relaxed enforcement of those laws) concerning so-called "victimless crimes." If you've ever been to Windsor or Niagara Falls, Ontario, you'll understand what I mean: their strip clubs are much wilder than the ones across the border in Detroit or Niagara Falls, New York.

A star quarterback for an NFL team located in a U.S. city on the Canadian border used to get stopped almost every weekend with a carful of Canadian prostitutes. The IIs dumped the girls and told the football player not to do it again or his car would be seized and he would be subject to other "severe penalties under the law." Of course, he never did stop trying to import whores because he knew nothing would happen to him because of who he was.

Big-time criminal gamblers and bookies can also be dumped at the border. The typical minor gambling violations don't count as CIMTs, but those guilty of "commercialized vice" are subject to exclusion. This section of the INA is aimed at organized crime figures, so it probably isn't likely to affect you.

DRUGS

I stopped working for the INS before an admitted pot smoker (but remember, he didn't inhale!) became Chief Executive, so I'm not sure if "The War on Drugs," in one form or another, is still being fought at the border. But I do know that drug offenses are the single largest reason why aliens are dumped on the basis of "Criminal and Related Grounds."

In inspectors' parlance, drug dumps are called "twenty-threes," and even a minimally competent inspector soon collects a lot of them. It's so easy because almost any violation of drug laws is a reason to be dumped. An alien can be dumped for anything from possession of an ounce of marijuana to trafficking in 10 kilos of heroin. The immigration law doesn't necessarily make a distinction, and a dump's a dump as far as an II's stats are concerned.

That's why inspectors will often ask about drug arrests, no matter how small, when an alien is sent to secondary for checks of other suspicions, such as CIMTs or having no work permit. Drug dumps are easy and common and inspectors are always on the lookout for them.

If you have even the smallest record for drugs and you're at all concerned about being dumped at the border, your concerns are probably not misplaced.

SECURITY EXCLUSIONS

Guarding America from aliens bent on assassinations, bombings, and similar nastiness is probably the most important (and perhaps the only legitimate) reason to station guards at the U.S. borders. But, in my experience, it's also the least likely business an inspector is going to deal with, no matter how long he serves on the line. Still, CIs and IIs take the national security aspect of their jobs very seriously. Few things would make the average inspector happier or more respected among his peers than to catch a spy or a terrorist. And "national security" can cover more possible exclusions than the layman is liable to expect.

Two examples of national security exclusions one might not immediately expect are Nazis and Communists.

Reds aren't excludable from the U.S. since ImmAct 90, but Nazis are. Of course, since no Nazis have been in power for half a century (and those still alive anywhere in the world probably can't travel to the toilet under their own power), it's unlikely that any II is going to stop one at the border. Nevertheless, Adolf Hitler was still in the INS lookout system in 1989—a hundred years after his birth, and 44 years after his death. I guess someone in Washington read the *National Enquirer* and decided it was true

that "they saved Hitler's brain." The Department of Justice still maintains an Office of Special Investigations (OSI), charged with hunting down Nazis. Under ImmAct 90, the category which covers Nazis was extended to include anyone "engaged in genocide." I haven't heard of any Khmer Rouge, Bosnian Serbs, or Rwandan Hutus kept out of the U.S. for that reason (or under investigation by the OSI), but I suppose it's possible.

Spies and saboteurs for hostile governments are more obvious targets for exclusion. On the outside chance that a copy of this book ends up in North Korea, Iraq, or Iran, I'd like to warn any spies that while the USCS and INS records can be haphazard on lots of subjects, they are very thorough on spies. INS records are augmented by the FBI, CIA, and Secret Service. I hope you get caught, Mr. Spy.

Terrorists may be differentiated from saboteurs by the fact that terrorists work for nongovernmental organizations, such as the Italian Red Brigades, the German Red Army Faction, and the Popular Front for the Liberation of Palestine. But they still blow things up, as the World Trade Center bombing demonstrated.

One terrorist case in which I took part, however, turned into a farce. It was Christmas Eve and I was working with a trainee inspector, trying to teach him the ropes on a night when almost no one was traveling. I inspected one alien traveling on a Lebanese passport, which made him an automatic secondary. I sent him to secondary, expecting nothing more to come out of the inspection than some pro forma paperwork before the Arab was on his way to the U.S.

After about 45 minutes, however, I noticed that the alien still hadn't left the secondary office and the supervisor on duty had joined the secondary inspector in questioning him. I left my trainee to guard the border that no one was crossing and went inside to see what was up. It turned out that the secondary officer suspected the Arab was a terrorist because of evidence in his luggage: a few innocuous Palestinian political pamphlets in English and a lot of stuff in Arabic (which, of course, none of us could read). The alien also carried photographs of himself standing with a microphone and apparently addressing enthusiastic crowds of Arabs.

Unfortunately, the alien spoke only Arabic and a little French but no English. We inspectors knew only a few words of French and not a word of Arabic. So the alien couldn't figure out why we were holding him up so long, and we couldn't really communicate with him well enough to determine if he was a terrorist or not.

Since we were at a big airport, it was ordinarily an easy task to find an interpreter, someone who worked for one of the foreign airlines who spoke Arabic. But it was Christmas Eve, few flights were scheduled, and the airport was almost empty of airline staff. Hours later, we found a security guard who spoke Arabic. He asked a few questions and found out that our "terrorist" was in fact a singer. The photographs that appeared to show political rallies were of the alien singing Middle Eastern pop songs. I asked him if he knew "Jingle Bells" and sent him down the road.

PUBLIC CHARGE

Aliens may be excluded from the U.S. as "public charges," or those who are deemed unlikely to be able to support themselves in the U.S. and, therefore, likely to become wards of the state or end up on perpetual welfare. As we all know, lots of illegal aliens end up on the welfare rolls. Why not, when they see all those native-born Americans living soft while sucking on the welfare teat? If you were an illegal from Mexico, China, Ireland, or someplace else, unable to work legally and maybe without marketable skills, mightn't you consider picking up some free dollars from the "social services" office?

Nota bene: If the politicians ever get serious about putting a stop to illegal immigration, they won't add the magical "hundred thousand new police" to the Border Patrol. Instead, they'll end welfare. Not "reduce" or "reform" or "end welfare as we know it." End it, period.

How many illegal aliens will continue to enter the U.S. once they realize that "there ain't no such thing as a free lunch"? Ending welfare will thin the huddled masses crossing the border and might also get a few million American citizens off their asses, out from in front of "Oprah" on the glass toilet, and back to work.

ILLEGAL ENTRANTS

It's easy to get confused on this one. "Illegal entrants" is a phrase used by the Immigration Service and, like most phrases dreamed up by bureaucrats and lawyers, it means something different from what it means in plain English.

To you, "illegal entrants" probably means anyone who enters the United States in violation of the law, such as the stereotypical Mexican who sneaks across the unguarded border at night in California or Texas. To the INS, "illegal entrants" are those excludable from the U.S. for certain very specific reasons, including having been deported, entering by means of fraud, or crossing the border as a stowaway or alien smuggler.

Deportees are usually not allowed to re-enter the United States until five years after the date of their deportation. If the alien was deported because of an aggravated felony, he is not allowed to re-enter for 20 years.

That sounds like pretty serious punishment—until you consider the fact that hardly anyone is deported from the U.S. (Don't confuse being dumped, which is "voluntary departure," with deportation. Deportation involves judges, jails, handcuffs, and leg irons.) Consider this: more than 25 percent of the prisoners in federal penitentiaries are aliens. Since all of those have been convicted of crimes, by rights they should all be deported. But the Detention and Deportation section of the INS doesn't have the manpower to deport that many aliens.

For some reason unfathomable to anyone but bureaucrats, the Department of Justice would rather hire "corrections officers" (what do they correct?) for its Bureau of Prisons (which is the fastest growing agency in the federal government, in case you're looking for a GS job) than add people to the Immigration Service, which keeps criminals from getting into the U.S. in the first place. Remember that tidbit the next time you hear the usual babble out of Sacramento and Washington about "getting tough on crime," "the need to build more prisons," and "dealing with our immigration mess."

Fraud is a clearer matter. Anyone trying to cross the border with a fraudulent passport or visa (two common reasons for exclusion on fraud), for example, expects trouble if he's caught. But even lying to an inspector about a minor matter can keep you from crossing the border. Inspectors quickly become experts at detecting lies, and they also soon learn that small lies often mask large ones—and thereby lead to dumps. At the very least, lying to an inspector is a sure way to make his job more difficult, piss him off, and decrease your chances of crossing the border.

From what I've seen, a lot of people hurt themselves by lying to inspectors over petty matters. The classic case came when I worked at an airport. There was a short line in front of my booth, and in the queue I saw a middle-aged man and a younger woman. By their body language and other signs, I could tell they were traveling together. But when it came time for their inspection, they went through separately. Both were Canadians from the same city, and both were headed to Miami for a week. The woman claimed she was on vacation. The man said it was a business trip. I knew that they were lying, so I sent them to secondary to sort out the facts.

After waiting in the crowded secondary area for more than an hour, and then going through interviews separately and together for another half-hour, it finally turned out that the man was going for a week's vacation in Florida with, as he put it, "a woman not my wife." Big surprise.

The man said he was "too embarrassed" to give me the real story on the line. He didn't stop to consider the fact that IIs are around to enforce the U.S. immigration law, not the Ten Commandments. I didn't give a damn with whom he went on vacation.

"Why did you lie to me?" I asked. "Now you're screwed." And screwed he was. First, he missed his flight because of the delay in secondary. Then, his mistress publicly broke up with him in the INS office and left by herself. Finally, in the course of the secondary inspection, a call was made to the man's wife, a co-owner of his business (where the mistress was employed as a "personal secretary"), and she hung up very suspicious. The man wasn't dumped by the INS, but he probably ended up divorced, without even a mistress to comfort him. He also missed his vacation. All because he lied to an inspector.

When your mother warned you that "honesty is the best policy," she wasn't kidding. At least it still is at the border.

I never dealt with a stowaway. They're pretty rare, and I doubt that any of them are reading this book. Anyone desperate enough to hide out in the bilge bottom of a ship or the unpressurized parts of an airliner usually comes from someplace like Cuba or Red China. If he survives his passage, he'll end up eligible for asylum. Anyone with the guts to get into the U.S. as a stowaway doesn't need my advice in order to beat the border.

Smugglers I have seen. Like everyone else who has ever guarded the border, I hate them.

Alien smugglers are scum. In the parlance of the border, alien smugglers are called "coyotes." Just like real coyotes, smugglers are half predator, half scavenger, and all varmint. Unfortunately, alien smuggling is a growth industry for the worst elements of organized crime.

For anyone foolish enough to believe a coyote is the way to beat the border, let me tell you a few true stories. On the Mexican border, CIs stopped a truck that gave off an awful stench, like rotting meat. In a hidden crawl space in the back of the truck were the corpses of a Mexican family. They had suffocated and were starting to rot in the Southwestern heat. The coyote driving the truck had a wad of bills in his pocket—payment from the Mexicans for getting them across the border.

On the Canadian border, a member of a Chinese triad (organized crime family) in Toronto collected $30,000 each from three citizens of Hong Kong eager to get into the U.S. before the Butchers of Beijing took over their island. The coyote put the people in a cheap rubber raft at night and sent them across the Niagara River—one of the swiftest and most powerful rivers in the world. The Border Patrol found the three drowned bodies the next day.

Never trust a coyote. He isn't interested in helping you to beat the border. He only wants your money. Once he has it, you're better off dead as far as the coyote is concerned.

DOCUMENTARY REQUIREMENTS

This category includes the single greatest source of dumps at the U.S. border. At first, that might not surprise you. Of course, you'll say, someone without the right documents, such as the correct visa, is going to run into problems at the border. And there are dumps under this category for both immigrants ("immigrants with wrong classification," as the INS puts it) and nonimmigrants without passports or the correct visas ("nonimmigrant without documents"). Most dumps due to documentary requirements, however, are the classic "illegal aliens." And there are lots and lots of them at every border crossing. They are every IIs meat and potatoes.

Properly, the INS terms such illegals "immigrants without an immigrant visa." That is, they are anyone who is not a citizen of the United States, lacks an immigrant visa (popularly known as a "green card"), but nonetheless lives and works in the United States and intends to go on doing so for a long time, if not permanently.

IIs sometimes still refer to anyone dumped for that reason as a "twenty"—because prior to ImmAct 90, they were excluded under section 212(a)20 of the INA. "Twenty" is a term inspectors will still use within earshot of an alien (they think you don't know what they're talking about, but now you do).

Unless you're a Mexican picked up by the Border Patrol in the Southwest desert, you're not likely to be called a "wet" or a "wetback" if you're suspected of being an immigrant without an immigrant visa. But it's a common term among IIs and CIs used on both the southern and northern borders (it always seemed especially popular at the INS Academy in Georgia), whenever inspectors are talking among themselves. Although "wetback" has become, in popular civilian speech, a derogatory term for Mexicans, it rarely carries any stigma among inspectors. It's just a term of the trade, and border guards don't really mean anything by it.

The peculiar fact about dumps of "twenties" is that they often occur after an alien has established a residence in the U.S. for a long time and has made repeated crossings of the border. Sometimes, an alien will be dumped because of having a one-way plane ticket and few demonstrable ties in his home country. At the land border, an alien is often dumped because of trying to carry all his worldly possessions across the border for a "vacation" in the U.S. But, in my experience, it's more common and easier to dump an alien with a record of repeated crossings. Invariably, he's complacent and, therefore, easier to catch.

Such longtime offenders are also invariably shocked to be caught. Twenties often think they have a right to re-enter the U.S. because they have a residence (illegal) and a job (also illegal) there. Inspectors are always more than happy to show them otherwise.

Aliens sometimes inadvertently slip into the category of "immigrant without an immigrant visa." I saw that happen when I worked on the Canadian border. Because the Canadian winters can be so harsh, a lot of Canadian retirees spend their winters in the southern U.S., especially in Florida. They're called "snowbirds." However, since a lot of those snowbirds own property in Florida, they eventually end up spending more than the winter in the U.S. One Canadian I inspected lived in Florida for eleven months of the year and only came home so that she didn't lose her government health insurance.

At the ports where I worked, the unspoken rule was to let the snowbirds fly, no matter how long they spent in the U.S. Sometimes we'd halfheartedly warn them that if they spent more than six months of the year (i.e., the majority of their time) in the U.S., they might run into trouble crossing the border "at some future date." For the most part, though, most inspectors didn't want to worry old ladies and men whose only "crime" was spending their pensions in the U.S. while they aged in the Florida sun. Nevertheless, come October and November when the snowbirds would be crossing the border in droves, gung-ho nitwits (remember Peter and Paul?) on the line would send a few scared septuagenarians into secondary until the rest of the IIs warned them to stop wasting time.

From an inspector's point of view, the good thing about dumping a twenty is that it's easy. Since the burden of proof is on the alien, an inspector can frequently dump anyone who isn't carrying proof of residence (e.g., a mortgage), proof of employment (e.g., months of back pay stubs), and similar things that no one crossing the border is liable to carry. Therefore, documentary requirements is a catchall category. If an inspector decides to dump an alien and can't find any other legitimate legal reason, he'll dump him as an "immigrant without an immigrant visa."

INELIGIBLE TO CITIZENSHIP

That's a polite way of saying "draft-dodger." Yes, draft-dodgers are dumped at the border all the time. It surprises the hell out of most of them, because they all think they're covered by Jimmy Carter's pardon. The Carter pardon, however, doesn't cover those who fled the U.S. to avoid Vietnam *after* they'd received an induction notice. The pardon also doesn't apply to deserters who were already part of the armed forces when they fled the country.

We used to dump plenty of "twenty-twos" (excluded under section 212(a)22 of the INA) at the Canadian border. The holidays were always prime time for these dumps because ex-Americans who had lost their U.S. citizenship due to draft-dodging would try to cross the border to meet their relatives in the U.S.

Thanksgiving was the top holiday for catching twenty-twos, because Canada celebrates the holiday in October (Columbus Day in the U.S.), and draft-dodgers will betray their American roots when they head to the U.S. for Thanksgiving in November. At some ports, the supervisors post lookouts the week before Thanksgiving so that inspectors can improve their stats by dumping draft-dodgers, or "Thanksgiving turkeys" as we IIs called them.

Don't expect a break from any II if you're a draft-dodger. Many inspectors are veterans, and more than a few served in Vietnam.

Deserters are bigger game. The army, the navy, and the rest of the armed forces like to catch deserters, so the INS lookout system at all border crossings has information on all deserters. The MPs will wait a long time to catch deserters. In the 1980s, there were still lookouts posted for deserters from the Second World War. That's how long they'll wait.

MISCELLANEOUS REASONS

Polygamists still cannot legally immigrate to the U.S., although they may visit. This provision of the INA is a carryover from the old days of the immigration law. Why the U.S. government—which seems to condone and even promote every kind of bizarre and perverse sexual activity nowadays—should continue to keep out polygamists makes less sense than most of the generally nonsensical immigration code. Keep in mind that one-fifth of the world's population, who are Muslims, are allowed by their faith to practice polygamy. Also recall the Old Testament patriarchs, who took many wives. The same U.S. government that won't allow polygamists to immigrate in the 1990s is the same U.S. government (but worse) that forced the Mormon Church to abandon plural marriage before it would allow Utah to join the Union in 1890.

If the government wouldn't throw out the pointless old, it did introduce something new and sensible with ImmAct 90: an exclusion for child abductors. Because of the profusion of divorce, custody battles, and child abductions you can read about every time you look at a milk carton, the Immigration Service introduced a penalty and lookout system for what it calls "international child abductors."

Inspectors tend to be very careful and persistent about investigating someone suspected of being a child abductor. CIs and IIs will grill an alien until hell freezes over if they have the slightest suspicion that he may be abducting a child. Most inspectors are working the dull government job they have for the sake of a regular paycheck to support their own kids, so you can guess how they're liable to treat someone they think might be kidnapping a child.

Men are much more likely than women to abduct children. Therefore, anyone traveling with a child—but men, especially—should always carry evidence that the child with whom they're traveling is their own son or daughter. They should also have permission (preferably written) from the child's mother that she has allowed the man to travel with the child. That's even more important when the man is divorced from the mother.

If you're a man traveling with children not your own (nieces and nephews, neighbor's kids, the Little League team, or whatever), make sure that you carry evidence that the parents have granted permission for you to be crossing the border with their children.

Remember, the burden of proof is on you. If you think there might be questions at the border, make sure you have the means to answer them. Such as what? Such as a note from the mother of the child with a phone number where she can be reached; birth certificates that show you are the father of the child; family photos that show you with the child and mother; custody papers from the court that grant you custody of the child.

Such evidence becomes even more important if the child with whom you're traveling is too young to talk. If the child can speak for himself, don't make the mistake of answering questions directed at him. Inspectors ask children directly for a purpose, and they want the child to respond. Whenever I inspected a man with a child, I always asked the kid, "Is this your dad?" If the answer was no, I made sure I found out what the relationship was and why the man had custody of the child.

Be prepared for questions that might seem too personal: "Are you the child's natural father?" "Where's the mom?" "Are you married to her?" "Divorced?" "Where are your documents to show that you have lawful custody and permission to travel with the child?" I asked a lot of those when inspecting men with children. I could be nice about it if I wanted to be, but I always made damned sure that I was satisfied with the situation, no matter how long it took. Most inspectors are the same.

212(a)34

You should recall that there were 33 reasons for which an alien could be excluded under the old immigration law. Those 33 reasons were, for the most part, carried over under the law as revised in 1990. Those are the official exclusions. The 34th represents the unofficial ones.

Every man and woman who wears the uniform of U.S. Customs or the Immigration Service has his own categories for the freaks, drunks, loudmouths, and troublemakers who may not be excludable from the United States under the law—but are nonetheless not going to cross the border as long as that inspector is on duty. I used to call this catchall category for anyone I didn't like and was determined to dump as "212 (a)34: Shithead."

Inspectors put people in that category for many reasons. Two stand out in my experience: drunks and obnoxious people.

Drunks range from rare to frequent, depending on which port is involved. At one place where I was stationed on the Canadian border, the bars were open three hours longer in the U.S. than in Canada. After the Canadian drunks had become blotto in their own country, they would head across the bridge for the U.S. For their own safety, we usually turned them around right on the line without any secondary inspection or formal grounds for exclusion. That procedure was, at best, extralegal (if not illegal), but it was practical and saved trouble for everyone. We stuck to it.

Obnoxious and insulting people usually tend to find their manners once they're in secondary, or even when an inspector plays Bad Cop on the line (I used to have a talent for that). Some people, however, never learn when to shut up. If you insult an inspector, then don't apologize and really make him mad, you're pretty much guaranteed to end up dumped—and maybe with a notation in the INS computer system that will cause you trouble every time you try to cross the border thereafter.

Two prime mistakes that loudmouths often make are racial insults and sexual slurs. Never call a black inspector a "nigger" or anything similar. Never use sexually insulting language against a woman inspector. If you get a Mary, you're liable to end up not just dumped but with your balls in a sling. Angry women can be unbelievably malevolent: the Indians didn't leave torture to the women for no reason at all.

I can say with assurance that a CI or II will step out of line and insult an alien without being provoked only on the rarest occasions. But it does happen. Even if it happens to you, however, you might consider letting discretion prove the better part of valor. Ignore it. After all, you just want to get across the border. Once you're across, send a complaint letter to the port director if you're still pissed off.

THE LAW OF THE BORDER

There's a law you'll never see in the immigration code. It's an unwritten law, but a law nonetheless. It rules the real world of the border. The law states: when in doubt, exclude.

For example, you may have been sent to secondary on suspicion of a CIMT. The inspector finds out that you were arrested in Canada for a crime that may or may not be the equivalent of burglary. He doesn't need to determine if the crime is, in fact, a CIMT, *because the burden of proof is on YOU*. The inspector will dump you, add to his stats, and tell you to bring proof that you're not excludable. What does he care?

If an II is mad at you and determined not to let you cross the border (something you will have avoided if you followed my advice), he may use inspectors' dirty tricks. He may just dump you as an "immigrant without an immigrant visa." Do you carry proof of established residence, employment, and similar ties to your home country outside the U.S.? Probably not enough to *satisfy the inspector*, which is what the law requires you to do. Another popular trick is for an inspector to say, "We have reason to believe that you have been arrested for a controlled substance violation" and dump you until you show up with a copy of a drug record you don't have.

People do indeed carry copies of their records. Aliens who have only minor criminal records (not drugs or CIMTs) sometimes carry a copy of their records in order to show the inspector that they are not excludable. I saw several Canadians who carried a printed record issued by the Royal Canadian Mounted Police. But remember that no II is *required* to accept your copy as proof of anything.

WAIVERS

If you are dumped, always ask the inspector if he can give you a waiver packet. Waivers are potentially available for almost every exclusion, including CIMTs and drugs (but not for Nazis, spies and terrorists, and child abductors). Waivers are supposed to be granted for pressing need or for old crimes from which you've reformed. More often, waivers seem to be granted because of money or political influence. I've inspected plenty of professional athletes and rock stars who had waivers for their drug arrests.

The waiver packet is a series of forms, including fingerprints. Once completed, you send it to the INS district office. Months later, some bureaucrat is liable to deny the waiver—but only after he has your prints and a lot of information to put into the computers.

Before you complete a waiver packet, you may think about whether it's worth the trouble and further sacrifice of your privacy. You may decide to take your vacation in Banff or Cancun instead of Disney World or Vail.

U.S. CITIZENSHIP

"U.S. Citizenship: Go For It"
—former INS advertising slogan

When you're at the border and trying to get into the United States, there's nothing better than to be a U.S. citizen. Nothing makes your border crossing easier than U.S. citizenship. If you're not a citizen by birth but can become one through naturalization, then do it. If you're a native-born citizen, don't even think about giving up your U.S. citizenship: you're guaranteed to regret it someday (and, fortunately, it's hard to lose U.S. citizenship). Once you are a U.S. citizen, carry the documents to demonstrate your citizenship to an inspector. There's no better way to beat the border.

GUARANTEED ADMISSION

Under the immigration law, only one class of persons is guaranteed admission to the United States. That class consists exclusively of U.S. citizens.

Note well that I said *only citizens*. Not residents. Not friends. Not allies. Not "green card" holders. Not aliens with jobs in the U.S. Not noncitizen spouses of U.S. citizens. Not visa holders. Only citizens of the United States have a *right* to enter the United States. All others enter as a privilege.

Rights are hard to take away. Privileges are easy to lose.

From the first day of their training, inspectors have this message drilled into their heads: only U.S. citizens have a right to cross the border. If you want to beat the border, you'll do well to pay just as much attention to that fact as do inspectors. Inspectors will be ready to dump anyone they can, but they dread the day they dump a U.S. citizen by accident. That leads to upset supervisors, pressure from the district office, regional office, or even (God forfend!) Washington, angry calls from congressmen and senators, a black mark on the Service, missed promotions, and ruined careers. Working as cogs in a bureaucratic machine, IIs fear nothing so much as those things.

Always keep in mind that the easiest—and the only guaranteed— way to cross the U.S. border is to demonstrate U.S. citizenship. If you are a U.S. citizen, *always* let the inspector know it.

WHO IS A CITIZEN?

There are two major ways by which one becomes an American citizen: birth and naturalization.

The Constitution is still the supreme law of the land, no matter what the judges and politicians who frequently ignore it might say and do. The Constitution grants citizenship by birth, specifically in the Fourteenth Amendment, which reads:

"All persons born or naturalized in the United States, and subject to the jurisdiction thereof, are citizens of the United States . . ."

The clause about being "subject to the jurisdiction thereof" is mostly a function that excludes the children of foreign diplomats born in the U.S. Otherwise, if you're born in America, you're an American. That's why you'll see so many Mexican mothers-to-be cross the border to have their babies in El Paso or San Diego. It's a perfectly legal (and pretty smart) thing to do.

Most everyone realizes that a baby born in the United States automatically becomes a citizen of the United States. But do you know what "the United States" means to the INS? The 50 states, of course, are included, along with Puerto Rico, Guam, the U.S. Virgin Islands, and the Northern Mariana Islands (scattered throughout Micronesia and including Saipan, Yap, and Truk).

Also, people born on ships within the three-mile limit, or within the halfway boundary on the Great Lakes, are U.S. citizens. I once inspected someone who claimed (correctly, it turned out) U.S. citizenship because of being born to foreign parents on board a ship near New Orleans. Had I stayed in the INS for 20 years, I probably wouldn't have encountered another such case.

Another way to gain U.S. citizenship at birth is through your parents. The Service calls this "citizenship by derivation." Derivation can become very complicated, depending on when you were born; the law used to change every five or ten years. Nowadays, the general rule to keep in mind is that if both your parents are U.S. citizens, you're a U.S. citizen, no matter your place of birth.

Citizenship by means of naturalization is one of the great things about America. Unless you're a pure-blooded Indian, your ancestors came to the United States from some other land. That doesn't make anyone any less an American. Becoming a naturalized citizen is pretty easy, too. One resides for three to five years as a "lawful permanent resident" (or "green card" holder), makes application, and takes an oath of allegiance, usually before a federal judge. Then you're as much a citizen as anyone born in Providence, Des Moines, or Albuquerque.

Although I use the shorthand term of "Immigration Service," remember that INS stands for Immigration and *Naturalization* Service. Naturalization is as much the business of the Service as is immigration. The INS wants and encourages people to become U.S. citizens. So if you can become a citizen, do so. As the INS taught me, "Citizen of the United States is the highest status in the hierarchy of terms." There's no better way to beat the border.

U.S. Citizenship

LOSS OF CITIZENSHIP

Losing U.S. citizenship is difficult. You have to want to lose it. Neither Congress, nor the INS, nor any other branch of the government can take away your citizenship, no matter how you obtained it. You have to give up your citizenship voluntarily. Moreover, losing your citizenship is like losing your virginity. Once gone, it's gone for good. As I learned from the INS training manuals, "Expatriation is irrevocable."

You've probably heard of the Seven Deadly Sins of the medieval theologians. There are also Seven Deadly Sins of U.S. citizenship—seven ways to lose your key to crossing the U.S. border. The INS calls them "the seven expatriating acts." They are:

- becoming naturalized in a foreign country
- swearing an oath of allegiance to a foreign nation
- serving in the armed forces of a foreign nation (unless authorized by State or Defense)
- accepting a post in the government of a foreign state, if that post brings with it foreign citizenship
- making a formal renunciation of citizenship before a U.S. diplomat in a foreign country
- making a formal, written renunciation of citizenship to the Attorney General during a war
- committing an act of treason

As you can tell, none of these acts are the sort we take easily or lightly. Officers of the U.S. government will do their damnedest to discourage you from giving up your citizenship, not least of all because they know from experience that you'll almost certainly live to regret it and will want it back someday.

A career Foreign Service officer I know once told me that he'd had three instances when Americans overseas tried to renounce their citizenship during the Vietnam/Watergate era. He always tried to talk them out of it and stalled (for days, if necessary) to keep them from going through with it. Once he failed, and, a couple years later, the ex-citizen showed up, wanting his citizenship back. By then it was too late. Inspectors look askance at anyone who has given up their U.S. citizenship. IIs, after all, deal every day with people desperately trying to sneak into the United States. Someone who voluntarily wants to get out of the United States strikes them as very strange. Most of those who perform "expatriating acts" are draft-dodgers like the Canadian "Thanksgiving Turkeys," or the sort of subversives whom federal law enforcement officers like CIs and IIs are not likely to welcome with open arms.

If you want to ease your passage of the U.S. border, don't ever give up your U.S. citizenship.

DUAL CITIZENSHIP

Dual citizenship most often comes about when a child is born in the United States (thereby automatically obtaining U.S. citizenship) to foreign parents, from whom the child derives the citizenship of his parents' country. The Immigration Service is ambivalent about dual citizenship. Dual citizenship can create complications for you (such as owing military service or taxes to two governments), but the U.S. government seems more worried that it's somehow not going to exact its pound of flesh from you. The Supreme Court, however, has expressly recognized dual citizenship as "a status long recognized in the law." So there's not much the feds can do about it.

As a person trying to cross the U.S. border as quickly and as easily as possible, there are a couple basic rules to keep in mind if you're a dual citizen. First, don't tell the inspector that you have dual citizenship until he asks you about it. You don't need to hide anything, but you also don't need to complicate things until necessary. Second, carry passports for both of the countries whose citizenship you possess. Then, on the primary line, show your U.S. passport to the U.S. Customs or INS inspector. Use the other passport to ease your entry into the other country.

U.S. citizens may possess another citizenship with any number of other countries. During my time on the border, I inspected

U.S. citizens who were also citizens of France, Haiti, Britain, Israel, Mexico, and, most often, Canada. At the U.S.-Canadian border, every inspector routinely encounters people who share citizenship with both nations, and he soon realizes that dual citizenship is no big deal. I even knew a couple of frequent crossers who had triple citizenship: American, Canadian, and Irish. Nationality law can get very complicated.

EVIDENCE OF CITIZENSHIP

From the point of view of the U.S. citizen traveler, one of the best things about the U.S. border is that *proof* of U.S. citizenship is not always required to cross the line. Most of the time, all the traveler has to do is convince the inspector, *to that inspector's satisfaction*, that the traveler is indeed a U.S. citizen. And then, it's "down the road."

When does a U.S. citizen need documentary proof of his U.S. citizenship? The first rule to keep in mind is that a U.S. citizen is not required by law to have any documents (passport, birth certificate, etc.) to demonstrate citizenship when reentering the country from Canada or Mexico. For once, the government has done the sensible thing in light of the fact that millions of U.S. citizens expect to easily cross their northern and southern borders whenever they want. Most of the time when a U.S. citizen reenters the U.S. from Mexico or Canada, especially at very busy crossings such as Niagara Falls or El Paso, he just answers the inspector's question, saying that he is a U.S. citizen. That's it.

If a U.S. citizen has visited some other country in the Western Hemisphere, whether in Central or South America or in the Caribbean Islands, he has to present some evidence of citizenship (e.g., birth certificate, naturalization papers) but is still not required by law to carry a valid U.S. passport. Nine times out of ten, however, he'll have his passport, often because the country he's visiting requires it. Only when a U.S. citizen has traveled overseas to the Eastern Hemisphere (Europe, Asia, Africa, Australia) does the Immigration Service demand that he present a current U.S. passport in order to re-enter the country.

Despite the rules that don't require a U.S. citizen to carry a passport, in the real world, there's nothing better to have in hand on the U.S. border than a U.S. passport. Your U.S. passport is the key to opening the door of the United States. Often, once an inspector looks at your U.S. passport, the inspection is over, you're in the United States and "down the road." So if you don't have a U.S. passport, then you might consider getting one. If you have a U.S. passport, then carry it.

Why not carry your passport? From the day I began working for the INS, I've always carried my U.S. passport when crossing the border. My hometown is only about 20 miles from three crossings between the U.S. and Canada. Around these parts, people are used to crossing the border all the time. Most of them don't worry about carrying evidence of citizenship. But whenever I cross the border, even if it's just to visit a Canadian restaurant for lunch, I carry my U.S. passport. I have yet to encounter a CI or II who asked for my passport. But if one does, I know I'll be ready to show it. Thereby, I'll simultaneously make the inspector's job, and my passage of the border, easier.

As a working II, I was always surprised by U.S. citizens who had passports but nevertheless didn't carry them when crossing the border. Some actually would say, "I'm afraid I might lose it." That makes about as much sense as leaving your car in the garage and walking everywhere for fear of an auto accident. A passport is a travel document. A U.S. passport is the ideal document to have when traveling at the U.S. border. Carry it.

Your passport can be a good document to carry even if it has expired. Passports are issued by the State Department. They are valid for 10 years as far as State is concerned. But as far as the Immigration Service is concerned, an expired passport is sufficient evidence of U.S. citizenship, as long as the traveler hasn't gone outside of the Western Hemisphere.

Working on the Canadian border, I inspected a lot of USCs (II talk for American citizens) who carried expired passports. Use common sense, though. If your passport photo is 20 years old and shows you as you looked 40 pounds and lots of hair ago, you might want to get a new passport and carry that when you're inspected.

U.S. Citizenship

There are a number of other documents that can prove, or at least demonstrate, U.S. citizenship. Some, such as the Coast Guard Mariners document (or "Z-card") are specialized and rarely seen at most border crossings. Others are frequently encountered by IIs and are the next best thing to a passport.

Chief among these citizenship documents is the certificate of naturalization. It's a full-size piece of parchment (suitable for framing!) with a photograph, seal, signature, biographic information, and various security features. Naturalization certificates are, therefore, very reliable evidence of both identity and citizenship.

The problem is how to carry a naturalization certificate. If you carry it unprotected, it can get wet, ripped, or otherwise damaged, just like any other piece of paper. Because it is so big, you have to fold it to fit in your pocket, and that only leads to creases and tears.

To avoid damaging their naturalization certificates, a lot of people carry a photocopy—usually because they fail to read the document, which clearly states that it is illegal to copy the paper! Don't worry if you've already copied your naturalization certificate: IIs aren't going to arrest you or fine you for making the copy. Instead, if you present a photocopy at the border, the inspector is going to point out that it is illegal to copy a naturalization certificate, and then tear up the copy in front of you. (I did that dozens of times.)

If you insist on carrying your naturalization certificate at the border, have sense enough to protect it with a waterproof envelope (*not* lamination, which destroys the seal and other security features) backed with stiff cardboard so it can't bend. Think as if you're mailing a valuable package via U.S. mail. Better yet, leave your naturalization certificate safe at home and carry a passport, which is both handier and more durable.

Birth certificates are another form of evidence you can use to demonstrate your U.S. citizenship. They can be good or bad. The chief problem is that they vary so much from state to state (or even from county to county) that there's no way for the inspector to determine the certificate's validity for certain. They tend to arouse, rather than allay, an inspector's suspicions of a false claim to U.S. citizenship.

Also, birth certificates are as hard to carry without damage as are certificates of naturalization. Some states issue wallet-sized birth certificates, and these are almost as good as U.S. passports on the border *when accompanied by a photo driver's license from the same state.* (Remember that a driver's license by itself has no bearing on citizenship; it only says that one of the 50 states allows you to drive a car there.)

Many U.S. citizens, preparing for a trip on which they'll cross the border, call up a travel agent or someone else who doesn't know how the INS operates and hears that a voter's registration card is good evidence of U.S. citizenship. As far as inspectors are concerned, however, voter's registration is almost worthless. They vary as much as birth certificates and are far easier to fake.

Worse yet, a dirty little secret of American politics is that many thousands of illegal aliens vote in U.S. elections. I have personally dumped wets who were citizens of Mexico, Haiti, and the Dominican Republic—and all were registered to vote in their illegal places of residence in the U.S. This will no doubt get worse with the "Motor-Voter Bill" nonsense, which hands out the franchise along with a driver's license to anyone, regardless of citizenship. Whenever you hear a politician from someplace with a high proportion of illegal aliens (such as Los Angeles, New York, or Texas) and that politician cries about how the United States government must not take measures to control its borders because of "rights," "fairness," and similar bullshit, you can be certain that the politician owes his office to the votes of wets.

Democracy has gone crazy; one doesn't need to be a U.S. citizen to vote in U.S. elections. Maybe we should start shipping absentee ballots to Mexico.

CUSTOMS INSPECTION

Immigration inspection for U.S. citizens—especially ones with U.S. passports—tends to be a quick and easy procedure. As far as most IIs are concerned, once they see a U.S. passport, the inspection is over.

CIs are another matter. U.S. citizens are not exempt a customs inspection. They can be subject to as in-depth an inspection as can any alien, up to and including a strip search or the dismantling of their car.

Most U.S. citizens who have a problem with U.S. Customs at the border, however, have it because of mundane matters. They think they can import any amount of alcohol or tobacco or similar items because of the mere fact that they are U.S. citizens. But Customs has strict laws concerning even citizens. If you have any worries about what you can carry back into the U.S. from a foreign country, pick up a current copy of a pamphlet "Know Before You Go," which the Customs Service issues for free. You can get them at border crossings or by calling the Customs office in the blue pages of your phone book.

Otherwise, the most common Customs questions concern how much money you're carrying. Don't be surprised if an inspector asks you if you're carrying more than $10,000. The $10,000 limit was imposed as part of "The War on Drugs." The plan was to reduce money laundering by narcotics dealers. How effective the plan has been in an age of electronic banking and quiet accounts in Switzerland, Bermuda, and the Cayman Islands remains to be seen. If you, the reader, are the type of person who carries $10,000 cash, I'd suggest that you purchase *many* copies of this book and distribute them to all your friends and relatives.

8

COMMON QUESTIONS

In the course of enforcing the law on the border, an inspector can ask you anything. *Anything.* And an inspector will ask you any question at all, no matter how prying, no matter how personal—if he thinks he needs to ask that question in order to complete the inspection to his satisfaction. What's worse is that you have to answer those questions if you want to cross the border.

As with most things on the border, however, there's little reason to worry about the questions an inspector is likely to ask during a real-world inspection. Because their job is so repetitious, inspectors tend to work on autopilot. They use a handful of common questions for most inspections, both primary and secondary. Your knowing how to answer those questions concisely, completely, and without ambiguity will make the inspector's job easier. It will also help you to avoid letting the inspection wander off onto tangents that lead to bothersome questions which you'll be obligated to answer if you want to beat the border.

OF WHAT COUNTRY?

If an inspector is running any inspection as he should, the first question you'll hear is, "Of what country are you a citizen?" Ninety-nine and forty-four hundredths percent of inspections begin with that question, or some variation of it. Variations range from a mumbled "Citizenship?" to the more common "What's yer citizenship?" to "Citizen of what country?" or anything similar.

But notice that I provided as the prime example, as the basic question of the border, the sentence, "Of what country are you a citizen?" That phrase is grammatically correct but it's also slightly awkward and unfamiliar. That's exactly what the Immigration Service wants.

The Service teaches IIs to use that phrase as their basic question precisely because it is somewhat unusual. Most aliens, when they cross the border, expect to be asked their citizenship, but not in the uncommon syntax of the INS. Therefore, if they have a prepared—and possibly false—answer ready for the inspector, the question gives them pause and better enables the inspector to get at the truth. The question is especially useful with aliens whose native language is not English.

You may doubt that something as simple and seemingly innocuous as the "Of what country . . ." question can be such a useful tool for IIs. But believe me, it works. I can recall dozens of aliens I caught making false claims by means of that question. Sometimes they were caught short and admitted their real citizenship before making the false claim:

"Of what country are you a citizen?"

Blurted out: "Canadian." Then a worried look, followed by, "I mean American." And from there, I had 'em.

Other times, the question would just lead to a puzzled look, a long hesitation, and then a false claim to U.S. citizenship. Too much hesitation always makes inspectors suspicious, and I found that the fundamental question I was taught as a rookie II lead to hesitation—and, eventually, to dumps.

WHAT ARE YOU GOING TO DO?

Once an inspector has determined your citizenship (which is usually a pretty easy task), he then has to satisfy himself that what you're going to do in the U.S. is legal under the immigration and customs laws. That can be a harder job.

Despite what you may have seen in the movies, inspectors never ask, "Business or pleasure." Never. It's a useless question for an inspector to ask. It also evokes an answer that answers nothing and can lead an inspector to think that you're being evasive. Save yourself some trouble and always answer the question the inspector actually asks in the real world, not the questions you've come to expect from the false world of movies and TV.

So what are the kinds of questions IIs and CIs are likely to ask in order to determine what you're up to in the U.S.? Usually the inspector will say something like, "What are you going to do in the U.S.?"

Don't just answer "Business" or "Pleasure" and expect to leave it at that. If you're on a pleasure trip, tell the inspector just what you're going to do. Be concise but be complete within the bounds of the question. For example, you may be going on vacation—but consider how many different things a person may be doing on his vacation. Put yourself in the inspector's place and realize that an answer such as "I'm going on vacation" doesn't tell him a whole lot. Better to be specific and say, "I'm going golfing at Hilton Head," or "I'm going to Disney World," or "I'm going gambling in Las Vegas." Answers like those will help the inspector, speed up your inspection, and help you get across the border. Vacationers and other people on so-called pleasure trips are easy inspections, in my experience. The aliens usually answer questions readily when they're on vacation.

Business trippers, however, sometimes answer questions about as readily as captured Resistance fighters in the hands of Nazis. The first mistake business travelers make is to think that an inspector cares about their business. I guarantee you, he doesn't. An II doesn't give a damn that your Beebusyness Corporation is secretly discussing a merger with the Antindustry Company. But he does give a damn that your business may be illegal under the U.S. immigration law.

Inspectors tend to ask business travelers a lot of questions because determining whether someone's business is legal under the INA isn't always easy. Oftentimes an alien will inadvertently slip from the status of a legal business visitor to one in need of a work visa. A very basic rule to keep in mind is that you'll need a work visa to cross the border if you are receiving a salary from a U.S. source. That's why inspectors will often ask you about the source of your salary.

Most business travel, of course, is perfectly legal. Inspectors know that and want you to tell them about it and thereby make the inspection easier for both of you. So instead of answering "business," say, "I'm going to our quarterly sales meeting at the head office in Dallas" or "I'm making a presentation to GM in hopes that they'll buy the windshield wipers my company manufactures." Just as with vacation travel, answers that combine brevity with specificity will help you to beat the border. Don't be afraid to give the inspector a thumbnail sketch of your business in the U.S., and don't be surprised if he asks a few more questions to convince himself that you're OK under the immigration law.

Inspecting business travelers is an art. Some inspectors can determine in one or two questions that an alien doesn't need a work visa. Others (inexperienced ones especially) take 10 minutes on primary, then send an ordinary businessman to secondary.

I learned to rely on two questions. First, "What company do you work for?" That question was useful at the port where I worked because a half-dozen companies sent through almost all the business traffic and never did it illegally. Second, "What will you do for that company in the U.S.?" That question usually led to explanations of sales meetings and other legitimate business. My business inspections tended to run smoothly and quickly. But be prepared for just about any questions from IIs and CIs if you're a business traveler. Keep cool and answer the questions completely and concisely, as I've suggested.

WHAT DO YOU DO FOR A LIVING?

This is a question that may be considered as related to the one just discussed. From an inspector's point-of-view, however, it has other uses. Even if you're going on vacation, an inspector will frequently ask what you do for a living.

Why? Two reasons.

First, an inspector wants to know that you do, in fact, *do* something for a living. If you have a job in your home country, it demonstrates ties that will tend to cause you to return to that country and not illegally overstay your admission to the United States. Also, a job shows the inspector that you have some means of support and therefore will not have to illegally seek work in the U.S. in order to pay for your vacation.

Second, knowing what you do for a living tells an inspector a lot about you. Do you have regular, honest work? Then the inspector tends to think that you're a reliable, law-abiding person. If you're on the dole, he may think differently. In subtle ways, an inspector can quickly tell if you're lying if he knows (or even pretends to know) something about your job. So, you're a chemist? What's Boyle's Law? You'd better be able to back up what you claim to be, even when answering seemingly casual questions.

Don't be afraid to tell the inspector about your job if he asks. Honest work is honest work, whether it involves bagging groceries at the supermarket, managing a Burger King, or teaching Russian literature at a university. Don't be ashamed of your job . . . in most cases, that is. Some jobs are red flags for inspectors on the border.

Lawyers are always a cause for concern. Most CIs and IIs just plain don't like lawyers (in that, they're like most everyone else). In parts, that dislike is due to professional jealousy: inspectors see lawyers making thousands of dollars for doing paperwork and steering through the maze of immigration and customs laws, even though the inspectors know more about the laws than the lawyers. Inspectors know that because of their training and specialized experience with the customs and immigration codes, they could easily do the job of lawyers—and make the same kind of money. But they can't. To do so would be "practicing law without a license." Because lawyers become politicians who make the laws, "practicing law without a license" is a crime.

More importantly, lawyers understandably tend to be very

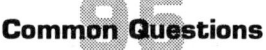

Common Questions

closemouthed about their business. Inspectors find that getting answers out of lawyers is like pulling teeth. During most of my inspections of lawyers, I usually ended up ready to knock out some teeth. If you're a lawyer crossing the border, be prepared for an extra dose of suspicion and maybe even a little hostility. And be ready for a lot of questions. Keep in mind the advice I've suggested all along: answer completely and concisely. And keep cool. You *have* to get past the inspector's questions in order to get past the border.

Entertainers can also expect an extra close inspection, especially if they're on vacation and don't have a current work visa. What exactly is an "entertainer"? The category covers movie stars, athletes, and models, but also strippers and call girls.

Therein lies part of the problem for an inspector. Legitimate entertainers require "O" visas ("O" for "outstanding ability"), and the good ones can usually get them easily. Sometimes, however, they don't want to wait for the paperwork and try to sneak through to a job in the U.S. by claiming that they're only on vacation. Viewing entertainers with an inspector's eye, you can see how easy it would be to work illegally in the U.S. if your work involves prizefighting, singing, or posing for a photographer. With the lucrative nature of such work, there's also great incentive for alien entertainers to lie to an inspector.

I have dumped, or have seen dumped, plenty of boxers, rock musicians, and models. So, if you're an entertainer going on vacation, be ready for plenty of questions, and be prepared to demonstrate that travel is all you're going to do in the U.S. If you're a legitimate entertainer going to perform, make sure you have a valid visa. If you're an entertainer in an illegal or borderline business, stay home or have a damned convincing story.

Consultants can also run into difficulties because of definitions. What exactly is a "consultant"? I can't define the term, and I know the INS never bothered to define it when I was working. That's why consultants can give IIs fits during inspections. An alien who visits a U.S. company for a week to offer advice on how to use a new phone system seems pretty clearly not to be working in the U.S. and doesn't need a visa. But how about one of the work-for-hire hatchetmen that companies use to fire employees during "downsizing"? Both might bill themselves as "consultants."

An important factor is the source of the consultant's remuneration. If he is part of a business in Canada from which he draws a salary and to which a U.S. business pays a fee for his services, then he probably doesn't need a work visa. But if he is paid a fee directly by the U.S. company, then he'll need a visa. Interpretations of the immigration law can be very tricky, and if an inspector is in doubt, of course he'll dump you. If you're a consultant, think about how you're going to explain your business clearly and concisely to an inspector, and have a plan before you cross the border. You'll thereby avoid problems.

Even if you're in a clearly defined trade, however, you can expect secondary and maybe exclusion if you carry the tools of your trade. Carpenters, plumbers, mechanics, and suchlike are frequently dumped because they try to drive across the border in the business van or with their toolboxes. They may claim to be on their way to Disney World, but how does the inspector know they're not going to work in the U.S.? If you're dumped for this reason, you'll usually be admitted once you return without your tools. But why not avoid problems and an entry in the border computer system by leaving the tools of your trade at home in the first place?

WHERE DO YOU LIVE?

Customs inspectors often begin their inspections with this question. Immigration inspectors are taught to never begin with the question, but they'll get around to it sooner or later in the course of most inspections. Where you live is important under both the immigration and the customs laws.

An II wants to know where you live so he can tell that you have a foreign residence to which you will return after your trip to the U.S. If you're a Mexican citizen, but your primary residence is in Houston, Texas, you'd better have a visa authorizing you to live in the U.S. or you'll be dumped. Citizenship and place of residence go hand in hand for the Immigration Service.

Common Questions

Customs Inspectors use your place of residence in a little different way. Even if you're a Canadian allowed to reside in the U.S., you can't import all the Canadian goods you want without paying the duties that other U.S. residents (citizens or not) have to pay. Also, CIs are on the lookout for the circumspect importation of cars. If you reside in a U.S. state, you have to register and license your automobile in that state, even if you are not a U.S. citizen. That means that you're going to have to import your car into the United States. Customs Inspectors are on the line to make sure you pay your fee to the U.S. Treasury for the "privilege" of doing so.

When an inspector asks you where you live, he means your primary residence, or "place of general abode," as the INS puts it. Many Canadians, for example, keep vacation houses in the U.S. but live and work for most of the year in Canada. So they can truthfully tell an inspector that they live in Canada. Sometimes, determining place of residence becomes more complicated, however. More about that when we deal with the next question.

HOW LONG WILL YOU BE?

Inspectors will usually want to determine the period of time you plan to be in the U.S. Like the previous question, this one has bearing on both Customs and Immigration matters.

The Immigration Inspector wants to make sure that you're not staying too long in the U.S. He needs to know, in effect, that, intentionally or not, you haven't become a "twenty," or an immigrant without an immigrant visa. Most travelers to the U.S. are admitted under the nonimmigrant categories of B-1 or B-2; that is, as visitors for business or pleasure. Normally, "B" admissions are made for six months, although an alien may be admitted for up to one year under the B category.

Problems start when an alien thinks he can stay as a visitor for a year, cross over to Juarez for a couple days, then re-enter the U.S. for another year. Sooner or later, you're going to get dumped and put into the INS lookout system (making any future entrance to the U.S. unlikely) if you try that trick.

Beat the Border

The general rule to keep in mind, even when you're not working in the U.S., is to stay at your foreign residence for at least six months and a day (i.e., more than half the year). Situations, such as six months in the U.S. year after year, can lead IIs to make judgment calls—and remember that an inspector's judgment is liable to come down on the side of dumping you.

Customs Inspectors want to know how long you're going to be in the U.S. because the length of your stay affects how much you may import. The number of cigarettes you can bring in without paying duty, for example, is not the same for a visitor on a weekend vacation to Las Vegas as it is for a student spending the semester at Princeton.

U.S. Customs also wants to know how long American citizens have been outside the U.S. If you want to bring back some Canadian beer from your trip to Toronto, it makes a difference whether you were there for a day or a week. The best source of information for U.S. citizens returning with goods from another country is the free pamphlet I've already mentioned, "Know Before You Go."

CUSTOMS QUESTIONS

It's impossible for me to give specific examples of many of the questions Customs Inspectors (or IIs serving as CIs under the system of dual inspection) might ask you at the border. Quite literally, they may ask about any of your goods.

They might ask you about the lunch you're carrying. Is that rice cooked? (Cooked rice can come in; uncooked rice cannot.) Where were those oranges grown? (Foreign-grown citrus fruits can't come into the U.S.)

They might ask about your pets. Has your dog had his shots? (Rabies is a problem.) Is that a parrot in that cage? (Parrots carry diseases and won't be allowed in without a lot of paperwork.)

There are hundreds of other matters that might be of concern to a Customs Inspector. In general, it's a good idea to have receipts to show what you bought outside the U.S. Also, if you're carrying something made in a foreign country that looks like it might be readily salable in the U.S. (e.g., jewelry, electronic equipment), then leave it at home—even if you haven't the slightest intention of selling anything. How does the CI know that? When in doubt, he'll charge you duty. Do you want to pay another tax?

9

HOW DO THEY KNOW WHOM TO STOP?

Chaos. That's just what the border may appear to be to the uninitiated. Travelers who seem ordinary go to secondary and maybe even get excluded from the U.S. Others, who seem like sure stops, get through. Someone who has crossed the border 20 times without incident is suddenly dumped. Another, who was dumped only last week, heads down the road. Are stops by border inspectors as random as they often appear?

No. Inspectors, of course, have the authority to send any traveler to secondary (if not necessarily to exclude them) for *any reason* that, in *his judgment*, applies. In the real world, however, all inspectors rely on a half dozen or so telltale signs when deciding who to send to secondary. Moreover, too many travelers create problems for themselves by demonstrating those red flags, deliberately or inadvertently.

Know the signs that are likely to get you sent to secondary or dumped. And avoid them.

GOOD MANNERS

Your mother was right when she told you to mind your manners. There's no better way to beat the border than by practicing the commonsense courtesies that should be second nature to any well-raised person. Unfortunately, in today's society fewer and fewer people seem to have been raised well. Consequently, a large number of people have rude behavior, not good manners, as their daily practice. Inevitably, that leads to trouble at the border. As an II, I was shocked by people who would respond to my questions with wise-ass answers or outright insults—and thought they could get away with it. They, in turn, were shocked to find themselves handcuffed to a chair in secondary or dumped on the flimsiest of grounds (whatever I could find). Surprisingly, ex-cons and hardened criminals almost always showed good manners (failing to show respect, I guess, tends to get you a shank in the liver on the inside). Middle-class snots and suburban punks who had never taken a punch tended to be the troublemakers.

The simple fact is that good manners ease your passage, while bad manners lead straight to secondary. Don't worry about being on your best behavior. Just use your common sense. For example, don't refer to the CI or II as "Hey, you." Call him "Sir" (or "Ma'am" for a woman inspector—there's no surer way to piss-off a woman in uniform than to call her "Sir") or "Officer" or "Inspector." Listen to the questions and answer them. Don't expect small talk unless he initiates it; remember, he has a job to do. Likewise, don't bother him with questions about directions, tourist sites, or where to find a bathroom, especially if the traffic is heavy. Don't be in a hurry to pull away; wait until the inspector finishes his inspection and signals you to go ahead. Have your documents (passports, visa, customs declaration) ready. In general, be cooperative, and be ready to help the inspector make your inspection easy for both you and him.

Such things, I hope, seem too simple for me to remind you about them. If so, you're already halfway to crossing the border without incident. But trust me when I say that a lot of people need such reminders.

Mind your manners even when an inspector is rude to you. That's rare (pretty rare, anyway), but it happens. CIs and IIs, as "meeters and greeters of the public," are taught to be polite, but some people are pure assholes, and for them no amount of training is going to stick. In case you haven't noticed already, those hired by the government haven't always been raised well.

More often, when you think an inspector is being rude to you, he's just harried. He has a million more inspections to get through, it seems, and he just wants to get you out of his booth. In such cases, especially, don't get into a pissing match you can't win. Cause trouble for an overburdened inspector and you cause trouble for yourself.

As an example, let me cite myself. I was on the line at 6 A.M. after five fitful hours of sleep the night before and almost a week of 12-hour shifts. The gallon or so of black coffee I'd guzzled to stay awake had enflamed one of my many gifts from the INS, an ulcer. That morning I'd bent over to tie my shoes and had pulled a muscle in my back, so I was in a lot of pain. It was the week before Christmas, and the line of holiday travelers I had to inspect looked endless. I inspected a USC (U.S. citizen) businessman with whom I was a little curt, too much so for his tastes. I finished the inspection and said, "Go ahead." He thought he'd crack wise and said with a voice full of sarcasm, "Merry Christmas to you too." That was a mistake.

"Stop right there, you son of a bitch!" I ordered. He froze.

I launched into a furious, foulmouthed tirade as I marched to secondary. He was scared enough to shit, and should have been. I was too overburdened and in too much pain to take any lip from the traveling public. My message to the secondary inspector: "Possible false claim. Nail him to the wall. Then thorough USCS—luggage, car, etc." A supervisor finally intervened and let the guy go, but not before he'd been frightened and delayed. When an inspector wants to screw someone, he'll find a way. Don't give him a reason.

How Do They Know Whom to Stop?

I have a temper. But better-controlled inspectors will sometimes use a little rudeness in order to provoke an alien into providing an excuse to send him to secondary. The inspector may have vague suspicions and wants to put the alien off guard, just like some fighters will talk to their opponents and provoke wild swings. Don't bite at the bait. Mind your manners at all times during an inspection, no matter what the inspector says.

STORIES THAT HANG TOGETHER

Few people are successful liars. Allegedly a few psychopaths, entirely without conscience, are able to lie without showing the slightest evidence that they are lying. But I haven't seen any, and I've inspected thousands of liars.

It's hard—maybe almost impossible—to lie completely convincingly to an inspector on the border. Whether you realize it or not, you give off telltale physical signals when you lie. Your voice quavers, your eyes shift, your hands shake. All those signs, and others, are little words of body language that let an inspector know the words coming out of your mouth are not true. Even if you think you're cold steel and always in control, you nevertheless give off such signs when you lie.

Sometimes those signs are so subtle that the inspector cannot tell just what they are. He may only have a vague intuition that you are lying. But he soon learns to trust his intuition. Consciously, he may not know just *why* he knows you're lying, but he knows you are. The gestalt of your words and body language during the inspection inevitably signals to an alert and competent inspector that you are lying.

Of course, it is possible to get away with lying to a CI or II, but don't bet on it. If you lie during an inspection, chances are that you'll end up being grilled in secondary, if not dumped.

The best way to beat the border, then, is to tell the truth. It may be morally good to speak the truth, but I'm giving advice that is wholly pragmatic. The purely practical fact in the real world is this: if you want to beat the border, then tell the truth.

If you have to lie, however, stick as closely to the truth as you can. Trying to fool an inspector with an elaborate masquerade is sure to lead to trouble. Be what you are. Act otherwise and you're sure to give yourself away, no matter how good an actor you think you are.

The best illustration of how elaborate lies will give you away is a case I witnessed and like to call "the Cocaine Priest."

On the primary line at a major international airport, a Catholic priest presented himself for inspection. As a rule, Catholic clergy get good treatment and quick inspections at the U.S. border (unlike a lot of countries where they are considered subversive to the local regime). The II in the booth saw the Roman collar and thought that he'd have just another perfunctory inspection.

Then he took a closer look. The inspector couldn't tell just why he felt this way, but he had a strong feeling that the priest in his booth was not, in fact, a priest. "He just didn't look like a priest," the II later said. And he was right.

Subconsciously, the II had picked up on the kind of subtle signals discussed above. The "priest" presented a Colombian passport that checked out, looked genuine, and the name on it came up blank in the INS computer. The II conducted his inspection in Spanish and asked the usual questions about citizenship, purpose of travel, and length of stay. The "priest's" answers were convincing and arose without hesitation.

Still the II had his suspicions. And so, he surprised the "priest" with a question remembered from his Jesuit high school education: "*Es presbyter?*" (Latin for "Are you a priest?") The inspector knew that any real priest of the Colombian's age would have studied Latin and would instantly understand the question. But the Colombian didn't have a clue.

After a long secondary, the true story came out. The secondary inspector found that the alleged priest not only didn't know a word of Latin but also couldn't answer basic questions about prayers and doctrine that any practicing Catholic, much less a priest, should have known. Once the IIs broke the Colombian, it turned out that the "priest" was a mid-level member of the Medellín cocaine cartel and was wanted by the DEA.

The Cocaine Priest thought he could beat the border because

of his disguise. Ultimately, however, the masquerade was so far away from the truth that it only gave away his true identity.

CLOTHES MAKE THE MAN (AND WOMAN)

The clothes you wear tell an inspector a lot about you. Body language can give away subtle signals, but the messages your clothes convey are more overt.

Keep in mind two rules for how to dress when being inspected. First, dress appropriately. Second, dress conservatively.

What is "appropriate" dress? Think about what you're going to tell the inspector, and dress as you would for that activity. Are you going to a business meeting? Then wear a suit and tie. Going on a Florida vacation? Your luggage better be full of shorts and bathing suits. Heading to Montana for trout season? An inspector will expect to find waders and a fishing rod among your things. You get the idea. If you claim to be going on a camping trip to the Grand Canyon but you're wearing a gray suit and rep tie while carrying a briefcase, the inspector is going to be suspicious.

How about dressing "conservatively"? Does that mean that every man should wear a jacket and tie and every woman should wear a skirt that covers her knees?

Of course not. But, again, use your common sense. If a woman is squeezed into a few square feet of Spandex, wears spike heels, and is painted like a streetwalker, she shouldn't be surprised if the inspector thinks she is one. If a man shows up with a shaved head, army boots, and a "White Power" t-shirt, the inspector is going to treat him like a skinhead. Both may seem like too obvious examples, but both are based on my genuine experiences. A foolproof rule is: dress in a way that *won't* make you stand out in a crowd.

A special note for women: if you have a sexy figure and are dressed to show it off, don't be surprised if you get *a lot* of attention from the male inspectors. That attention may even extend to sending you to secondary (so that everyone in the office can get a look). If something like that happens to you, don't get upset. Take it as a compliment. It's just another way inspector's break up the monotony of their job. Such behavior may be terribly "sexist," but it's the way of the world—at least on the border.

Another tip, related to the advice to dress appropriately, is to dress for the weather. In other words, don't wear a down jacket in July, or shorts and a tank top when it's snowing. I once saw an II catch an alien crossing over from Canada on foot at the Rainbow Bridge in Niagara Falls. It was March, which can still mean wintery days in that part of New York State. But there had been a sudden heat wave that day, and all the other travelers on the ped line were in their shirtsleeves. The suspicious alien, however, was wearing an army coat buttoned to the neck. Underneath he'd stashed a half dozen bottles of liquor, which he thought he could sneak in without paying duty. U.S. Customs convinced him otherwise when the II on the line sent the alien to secondary. Later, when I asked the II how he'd spotted the secondary, he said, "He wasn't wearing that coat to keep warm."

The same rule that applied to the stories you tell an inspector also applies to physical appearance. It's hard to hide what you are.

One good example of that fact is the "con look." Men who have spent a lot of their lives locked away in prison tend to take on a distinctive appearance. Being indoors in a cell most of the day, smoking a lot (as most prisoners do), and, perhaps, the penitentiary diet and stresses of incarcerated life give many ex-cons something called "prisoner's skin" or "prison pallor." Also, the body language one picks up after a long time "in the joint" often sticks with a person after he's free. Inspectors learn to look out for such signs.

A very sharp woman II with whom I worked once sent to secondary two aliens on their way to a Florida vacation with their wives. She had no information from their answers on the line or from the INS lookout system that they had criminal records, but she sent them in for record checks anyway due to a vague suspicion that her years of experience had taught her to trust. It turned out that both aliens had long records and each had done more than 10 years in prison—something not even their wives knew. Of course, both were dumped for CIMTs.

How did my colleague know to send them to secondary? I asked her, and she said, "They just looked hard."

Whether you're aware of it or not, your clothes and looks are likely to give away your true background to border inspectors.

There are a few steps you can take with regard to your appearance that will help to keep you out of secondary. In addition to the advice about clothes I've suggested already, you should avoid like the plague three other things that may arouse suspicion.

One thing to avoid is the "dirtbag" look. Good grooming can be as useful as good manners. If you're a man with a ponytail and scuzzy beard or a woman with a shaved head, you can expect extra suspicion. Many IIs and CIs are straight-arrow types, clean-cut (regulations of the Immigration Service and U.S. Customs require it), and often ex-military. Naturally, they'll have a soldier's contempt for "long hairs." As far as most inspectors are concerned, the law-abiding accountant on legitimate business isn't going to look like a dirtbag, but the potential dump is.

Some inspectors are finicky about sunglasses. An II from whom I learned a lot always made everyone who came into his booth wearing sunglasses take off the shades. He wanted to see their eyes. That was a good procedure which I learned to follow; I noticed many other inspectors used it. For one thing, some aliens using false ID try to disguise their appearances with sunglasses. Also, drug users with dilated pupils often try to hide their condition by means of shades. Finally, the eyes are one of the primary giveaways if someone is lying, so inspectors always like to get a good look at your eyes. If you're wearing sunglasses, my advice is to take them off before you step into the inspection booth.

Tattoos aren't so easy to remove. If you have tattoos that are readily visible and mark you as an ex-con, you'd be smart to stay home. Inspectors have access to lookout books that indicate tattoos for prison gangs, such as the Mexican Mafia and Aryan Nation. Don't think that because you picked up a prison tattoo in a foreign country that a U.S. border inspector isn't going to know what it signifies. I was on the line when an II dumped a green-card holder because of an armed robbery conviction in Cuba. How did the inspector know? Because of the small tattoo on the web of skin between the Cuban's thumb and forefinger. The II had been studying the INS intelligence bulletins, which showed such tattoos. If you picked up tattoos in the navy or someplace similar, don't worry. But don't be surprised if an inspector asks you about them.

HANDS AND FIDGETING

As mentioned above, one of the words of body language by which inspectors become suspicious of an alien's answers is trembling hands. Nervous gestures, such as pulling on the fingers or cracking knuckles, are other suspicious signs. Fidgeting in other ways (shifting weight from one foot to another, squirming in the seat of your car) may also cause an inspector to suspect you're hiding something.

The problem with such signs is that they're not at all foolproof. Some people—even a majority of them, in my experience—get at least a little nervous when confronted by an authority figure in uniform. Inspectors expect a certain amount of nervousness from the traveling public (and a few inspectors are natural hard cases who inspire fear without trying). Should an inspector ask you why you're acting so nervous if you have nothing to hide, don't be ashamed to tell him that you're subject to the shakes around police and other authority figures. Blame it on your grammar school principal. You may ease the inspector's suspicions.

One vital note to bear in mind about your hands: if you're driving across the border and an inspector suddenly tells you to keep your hands on the steering wheel, then *DO IT!* He may think you have a gun in the car. If you don't comply with his orders, you're liable to end up with lead poisoning of the .357 kind.

I was in my booth once, inspecting a Canadian crossing the bridge to get gas (which is cheaper in the U.S.). I thought I saw a pistol half under the floor mat on the passenger side. I shouted, "Keep your hands on the steering wheel," as I hit the silent alarm with my left hand and put my right on the butt of my revolver. The pistol in the car turned out to be a water pistol (but very realistic-looking from a distance) that the Canadian's kid had left in the vehicle. But if the man hadn't had sense enough to do as I'd told him, who knows what would have happened? It gave us both a scare—me a minor one, him a huge one.

WATCH WHAT YOU CARRY

The things you try to carry across the border can, of course, get you into trouble with U.S. Customs. But do you realize that the things you carry can also get you dumped by the Immigration Service? Be aware of what you're carrying—especially in your car. Narcotics are things for which every inspector is always on the lookout. Druggies are stupid (why else would someone willingly put poison in his body?), so warnings I could give the drug users would probably be wasted. For the rest of my readers, let me tell you a couple true tales of just how stupid druggies can be when crossing the border.

If you were driving your vehicle across an international border, where an armed officer of the U.S. government was certain to inspect you, would you have a reefer in plain sight in your car ashtray? Well, mind-numbed drug users have done just that four times in my inspection line.

Once, the dope didn't even have sense enough to put out the joint: it was burning in the ashtray as he pulled up to my booth. He rolled down the window, and I could smell the pot smoke. I didn't even bother with the citizenship question. "What's that in the ashtray?" I asked.

"Just a cigarette, man."

"Looks like a joint to me."

"Huh?" the stoned alien replied. And that pretty much summed up his state of mind. We not only dumped him but also seized his car under the "zero tolerance" program then in force.

U.S. Customs watches for pornography. *Playboy* and *Penthouse*, or their foreign equivalents, won't cause any difficulties. Problems arise, however, when something stronger is in your luggage. The kind of photos that wouldn't raise an eyebrow in Denmark may put you in handcuffs on the U.S. border. Sometimes IIs will use pornography on your person as a convenient, if unofficial, excuse to dump you. Beware especially of homosexual pornography. If your tastes run to kiddie porn or something equally disgusting, you're liable to end up handcuffed to a chair in the back room where IIs take batting practice with their flashlights before you're dumped. A general rule about pornography: if in doubt, leave it out.

It's easy to violate the customs laws without meaning to do so. Items you think innocuous may not be so to Customs Inspectors. Aliens frequently are surprised to have their oranges, tangerines, or other foreign-grown citrus fruits seized at the border. Never carry citrus products when applying for admission at the U.S. border. You may be let in, but the citrus won't. The U.S. government is afraid the diseases that foreign citrus can carry might infest the U.S. crop.

Animal products can also cause problems. There is an international treaty banning ivory products (designed to preserve elephants), and the United States is a signatory. CIs will therefore be on the lookout for *anything* made with ivory, such as pocketknife handles, chess pieces, or jewelry. Inspectors will seize the ivory at the border and may fine or arrest you—whether you were aware of violating the law or not. Beware of *any* animal products you buy in Africa or Third World Asian countries: they may be made from endangered species and can be cause for trouble with U.S. Customs.

The INS may also be interested in the things you carry. Often, the goods an alien brings across the border are admissible under the customs laws, but those same goods tip off the IIs that the alien is in violation of the immigration code.

The classic case (and one I've seen repeated many times) is the alien dumped as a "twenty" because of going-away cards discovered in his luggage. The alien claims to be going to the U.S. for a short vacation, but in secondary the IIs find cards that wish the alien good luck in his "new life and new job in America" (TRUE! I read that on a going-away card). If you're planning to live and work illegally in the United States, leave the "best wishes" in your home country.

AUTOMATIC SECONDARIES

No matter how carefully you mind your manners, dress appropriately, and pay attention to what you carry, you can still end up in secondary just because of who you are. On the border there are certain categories of people who will always be subject to especially close inspection.

First of all, be prepared for secondary if you're a citizen of, carry a passport from, or are even a U.S. resident ("green card" holder) originally from one of the countries designated by the State Department and the Immigration Service as "special interest countries" (SICs). The list changes from time to time, depending on who is on the U.S. government's shit list. The SICs I recall from my days as an II included Iran, Iraq, Jordan, Lebanon, Libya, Syria, Tunisia, and Yemen. Nowadays, North Korea is probably also on the list, as is Sudan. As you can guess, the "special interest" the U.S. government has in SICs has to do with state-sponsored terrorism.

Don't worry if you're from a special interest country. As long as you're not a terrorist (and I don't expect you are!) and your trip to the U.S. is legal, you'll be admitted. Don't get upset and think that you're being singled out for harassment. Remember that the inspectors are just doing their jobs. A special interest secondary is routine for IIs and usually consists of a few extra questions, a closer inspection of your documents, and, perhaps, an extra computer check.

Arabs, or travelers from other Muslim countries such as Afghanistan, can expect a close inspection even if they're not from a special interest country. That may seem terribly unfair and prejudicial, but, from an inspector's point of view, it's only common sense. After all, it wasn't Canadians who bombed the World Trade Center or labeled the U.S. the "Great Satan." Don't get pissed-off. Instead, keep calm, expect delay, answer questions completely and politely, and you'll get by just fine.

Prejudice may also seem to be involved when people from West African countries are sent to secondary—as they invariably will be. U.S. Customs will be especially interested in aliens from countries such as Ghana, Liberia, and, in particular, Nigeria. Statistics compiled by the Customs Service show that much of the heroin smuggled into the United States is carried by organized gangs of Nigerian criminals. Nigerian-based organized crime is also heavily involved in credit card fraud and the importation of endangered species. You may be from Nigeria and the most honest and law-abiding person alive, but how does the inspector know that until he inspects you? Expect extra attention at the U.S. border if you're from a West African country.

There's a bumper sticker which reads, "Being a biker is not against the law." Well, that's true. But in the real world you can expect secondary if you're a biker trying to cross the U.S. border. The biker look—leathers, beard and long hair, tattoos—is, like the dirtbag look, a case where your appearance can cause you trouble. That may be prejudiced, but it's a sound prejudice on the level of staying away from dogs foaming at the mouth. Inspectors know that most bikers are just people who like to ride Harleys. They also know, however, that Hell's Angels and similar biker gangs are organized criminals who control the amphetamine trade and traffic in arms. Since criminal bikers are usually armed and prone to violence toward police, inspectors will be particularly careful around them. If you're a biker who looks like a biker, keep your hands in plain sight when you're at the border and be ready for a closer-than-average inspection. An inspector is not going to play games with his safety in order to keep from hurting your feelings.

Men traveling with small children can expect, at the least, a thorough primary inspection. They may well be sent to secondary. Reread the section on exclusions for child abductors for the reasons why.

In addition to the predictable and automatic secondaries I've already mentioned, almost every inspector sooner or later develops peculiar prejudices. There's no predicting those. For example, I would have inspected every Japanese who came through the port because I found them to be polite and patient without fail. One of my colleagues, however, hated "Japs" and always gave them an extra-long inspection. Another II did the same thing to every Jamaican who came into his booth. Should you run into an inspector with such peculiar prejudices, there's not much you can do other than bear with it. Keep cool until you've beaten the border. If you're still mad afterward, send a complaint letter to the port director or the district office.

LANE CHANGING

Once you're in a line in front of one inspector's booth, stay in that line unless another inspector waves you to the open booth. I've found that drivers at land borders are especially prone to shift from lane to lane. That's a mistake. When you change lanes without being told to do so, an inspector is likely to think that you're trying to avoid his inspection for a reason. He may suspect you have something to hide and that you're trying to avoid a close inspection.

Most of the time, lane changing is an innocent mistake, but the inspector doesn't know that until he's finished his inspection—usually one more thorough than it would have been had the alien stayed in one lane. Fortunately for the reader who wants to cross the border as quickly and painlessly as possible, lane changing is a mistake that's easy to avoid. Just don't do it, and you'll beat the border that much more easily.

10

DOCUMENTS

Real and Fake

Bureaucracies love paper. A bureaucracy will gladly produce a document for any need or desire, real or imagined. Why not? Government bureaucracies, after all, don't really have to pay for all the paper they produce. The government doesn't pay for things with so-called "government money" created out of thin air: it pays with money taken in taxes, taken from you and me.

That's why government bureaucracies are so free to multiply documents. There is more paperwork on the U.S. border, it always seemed to me, than anyplace else on earth.

The INS is, perhaps, the most persistent offender. I could devote an entire book to just the documents and forms of identification issued by the Service and used on the border.

But you don't need to know everything about documents in order to beat the border. In this chapter, I'll introduce you to the documents most commonly encountered at the border. I'll also recommend the best ones to carry and explain how crooks forge documents—and how inspectors spot them.

NEVER TOO MUCH EVIDENCE

For a person, alien or U.S. citizen, trying to cross the U.S. border, there's no such thing as too much evidence.

As I've recommended throughout this book, consider the situation from the inspector's point of view. When a CI or II is on the line and trying to determine within a minute or less whether you, someone the inspector has never seen before, are admissible to the United States, he can take one of two actions. He can take your word that everything you tell him about your citizenship, place of birth, residence, and reason for going to the U.S. are true. Would an alien eager to get into the Land of Opportunity be so dishonest as to lie to an officer of the U.S. government? Or, the inspector can study the passports, alien resident cards, or other forms in your possession that provide him with cover-your-ass-assured *documentary evidence* that you are who you say you are and are doing what you say you're doing.

If you were an inspector sworn to guard the border (and paid to do it), where would you place your trust?

Of course, you'd want to see the documents. You'd also want to see as many of them as you could get your hands on. Documentary evidence is like gold at the border. The right documents make an inspector's job so much easier. And, therefore, documentary evidence will also make your passage through inspection at the border easier and faster.

That's why I recommend that even U.S. citizens who were born and raised in the U.S. and "look American" nevertheless carry a U.S. passport when crossing the border. The inspector on duty may never ask to see the passport—but if he has any questions about your citizenship, there's no better way to answer them than with that ideal travel document, the United States passport.

If, for any reason, you suspect that you may have some difficulty convincing a CI or II that you're OK to cross the border, then prepare to meet the challenge. Prepare the documentary evidence in advance. Learning to think like an inspector, as I've emphasized throughout this book, should help you to do that.

Let's say, for example, that you're a Canadian citizen, born in India, who is taking an extended trip of six months in the United States. Because you know what inspectors look for, you suspect you might be refused admission to the U.S. as a "twenty," or someone going to live and work in America without an immigrant visa. What should you do?

First, carry your Canadian passport. The photo and biographical information will establish your identity. The document will also tell the inspector that despite your East Asian looks, you are a citizen of Canada and therefore do not require a visa to visit the U.S.

Second, have some evidence that you plan to leave the United States. If you're traveling by plane or train, for example, a return ticket will help to convince the inspector that you don't plan to take up residence in the U.S. An itinerary of the places you'll visit in the U.S., hotel reservations, and that sort of thing might also be helpful.

Third, have evidence of your roots in Canada and of financial support. A letter authorizing a leave of absence from your job or school might help the inspector to know that you're not a tramp wandering from one country to another. A bank book with a balance of a few thousand dollars back in Canada would indicate to the inspector that you have the means to afford a vacation, and that you have something to which you'll return at home.

By now I'm sure that you have the idea. You probably can think of other pieces of evidence that could be of use in convincing an inspector that you're legit. It's possible, and even likely, that an inspector on the U.S. border might never look at more than the passport—but if he does ask for more evidence and you can't provide it, you're going to end up in secondary and/or dumped at the border.

FORGED DOCUMENTS

The simple fact is that it's hard to fake documents well. At

Documents

least in my experience that's the case. U.S. ports of entry always keep some examples of the forged documents their employees find so that all the inspectors may study and learn from them. Therefore, even though forged documents found at the border are not common, I have probably seen at least a hundred various types. During the course of my career with the INS, I caught a few myself. In all but a handful of cases, the forged documents I've encountered were of poor quality. (Of course, that may only mean that the good forgeries got past us inspectors.)

Most of my experience has been with documents issued by the Immigration Service, such as the ubiquitous "green cards." INS documents designed to be carried as ID at the border have at least a dozen security features, ranging from seals and special marks in the printing to legends that appear only under black light. Inspectors must know all the security features on all the common INS documents before they're allowed on the line by themselves. As a rule, I was taught to identify at least three points of every document right there on the line.

Even the visas stamped onto the pages of foreign passports by the State Department have eleven security features that an II or CI can readily identify on the line. In fact, the U.S. visas in passports are often of much higher quality than the passports themselves.

Passports vary widely in quality. U.S. passports, as I've emphasized already, are the ideal documents to have on the U.S. border. Understandably, U.S. inspectors are going to be most familiar with the security features on a U.S. passport, and therefore they'll be quickest to identify the document as genuine. Conversely, U.S. inspectors will have an easy task at catching forged U.S. passports as fakes—so be warned if you're considering using a forged passport to beat the border.

U.S. passports have lots of security features, and, in general, are of high quality. They are also hard to tamper with successfully. Canadian passports are also of universally fine quality and have the bonus of having security features with which a U.S. inspector, especially one who works on the northern border, will be familiar. Of course, that bonus becomes a hazard to an alien using a forged Canadian passport.

Other high-quality passports include Japanese and Western European ones. More and more, the passports of the individual European countries, such as Britain, France, and Germany, are giving way to the European Community passports, which are easy for inspectors to identify as genuine and are of good quality. Passport quality tends to slip away rapidly after those countries. Passports of Third World countries, especially those of sub-Saharan Africa, are of notoriously low quality and easy to forge. But that isn't much of a concern for IIs. Who, really, would pretend to be a citizen of Malawi or some such place?

Still, don't think that it's easy to fool U.S. inspectors with forged passports from such countries or ones that have been tampered with. Every port has a big book called "The Passport Identification Manual." The book contains color photos of passports from every country in the world, as well as the various security features of the documents. The manual is very thorough and is frequently updated.

As much as I've warned you about the difficulties of producing high-quality, or even competent forgeries, real professional counterfeiters can sometimes do remarkably good work. The ingenuity shown by skilled forgers can even impress inspectors.

The foremost example of forgery I ever encountered involved a Japanese passport. The bearer was in fact Chinese and was using the fact that Japanese tourists don't need visas as a way to get into the U.S. and take up illegal residence. Japanese passports are of good quality and therefore are hard to counterfeit. But the organized alien smuggling ring that had supplied the passport (for $35,000) had solved that problem by using a genuine passport stolen from its Japanese bearer.

The trick was how to get the information about height, weight, and the rest to match the new bearer, who was considerably different from the true Japanese owner. To remove the printing without damaging the information page, the forgers smeared the appropriate letters with peanut butter. Then, they left the passport open in a cage full of cockroaches. The bugs ate the peanut butter—and at the same time ate the ink of the letters printed on the page *without damaging anything else.*

Documents

Then, they simply reprinted the correct information. The substitution was flawless except under close examination with a microscope. We in the INS would never have identified the passport as one that had been tampered with if the Chinese bearer hadn't gotten cold feet and ratted out the whole scheme.

The chief reason why it's wise to avoid using false docs is that they can lead to severe penalties if they're found out. An ordinary "twenty" caught on the border is just going to get dumped. But a "twenty" using a counterfeit passport is going to be arrested, fined, and deported. Think of the difference as that between a traffic ticket and a felony. The risk, of course, is yours, so think carefully before using shady documents to beat the border.

Another danger to keep in mind is that forgeries tend to be overpriced. Most fakes, as I've said, are of poor quality, and the prices wets pay to get them are rarely commensurate with the merchandise. From interviewing aliens, I learned that forgers charge prices of $500 to $3,000 for fake green cards and passports that any inspector who is not in a coma will detect in an instant. Amateur forgeries are even worse.

Quality workmanship costs big money and requires unusual resources. That's why the kind of fake documents that are likely to fool most inspectors are used by spies, high-level members of organized crime, and other such pros. If you're a spy or Mafia boss reading this book, though, none of what I have to say is news. For anyone else with the connections and money, expect to pay $10,000 or more for fake documents in which you can put some trust. But if you can pay that much for a fake green card, you can probably afford a slick immigration lawyer who can get you into the U.S. legally.

From an inspector's point of view (and always keep in mind my advice that the best way to beat the border is to adopt that viewpoint), false documents aren't much of a problem. Indeed, looking for and, better yet, finding false docs can be an inspector's greatest joy in a notoriously dull job. Therefore, if an inspector has even the slightest suspicion that your documents may have been forged or tampered with, he will study those docs as long as he deems necessary to convince himself that they're genuine. He'll also invite his colleagues to get in on the fun. At one port where I worked, even the port director, who never did inspections, would leave his office to study possible fake documents. He was good at it, too.

The Immigration Service usually provides its officers with plenty of tools to detect false documents. A lot of inspectors carry magnifying glasses to use right on the line. In secondary, most ports will have black light machines, high-powered lighted glasses, and microscopes. Some have more sophisticated equipment, such as the Photophone. The Photophone is a kind of superaccurate fax machine which allows IIs to transmit images of suspect documents to INS headquarters. There, the technicians can study the docs more closely. You may also find that newer passports can be read by a machine right on the line, and fakes or passports that have been tampered with set off an alarm.

With all those means of finding false documents, it's important to avoid having your genuine document give the appearance of a counterfeit. For example, illegals often try to pass off low-quality fakes as just battered and worn documents. Inspectors are liable to be suspicious of torn, dog-eared passports with faded pictures and peeling seals. Take care of your documents so that they retain the appearance of the real things.

IMMIGRATION DOCUMENTS

INS offices at the ports of entry where I've worked maintain a file of the many documents the service issues. The file fills four or five drawers at one copy each—i.e., an entire cabinet. Frankly, there are far too many immigration forms. Even longtime IIs aren't likely to see all of them. Fortunately, however, the average traveler needs only be concerned about three: passports, so-called green cards, and the ubiquitous I-94.

I've already discussed passports, so we can turn to "green cards." If you have a green card or have ever seen one, the first thing you'll notice is that they're not green. Recent ones are basically pink, or "salmon-colored" as the INS phrases it.

So how did the name "green card" come about? Until the Second World War, there weren't any such documents for aliens

residing legally in the U.S. After Pearl Harbor, however, the same U.S. government that locked native-born Americans of Japanese descent in concentration camps decided that all resident aliens were potential spies and saboteurs and therefore had to carry a card as a means of identification and state control. With the printing technology of the time, green inks were considered the most secure (something that survives in U.S. paper "money"). So, from the 1940s to 1972, the cards issued to resident aliens were, despite 15 revisions in design, generally green. The name "green card" just stuck after the appearance of the document changed.

In popular slang, even inspectors still use the term "green card." However, IIs use in their memos and around each other the proper designations for the document: I-151 (for the pre-1972 design) and I-551 (for the newer ones).

Just what is a green card? It is a wallet-sized immigrant visa. It demonstrates that the bearer is a resident alien of the United States, one who is legally allowed to reside and work in the United States on a permanent basis. It signifies nothing more and nothing less.

By that I mean that *A GREEN CARD DOES NOT GRANT U.S. CITIZENSHIP*. Keep that in mind. Never claim to be a U.S. *citizen* on the line, and then produce a green card. There's no surer way to piss off an inspector. You might end up in secondary, and you'll almost certainly get a lecture about the meaning and importance of U.S. citizenship.

Since a green card does not grant you U.S. citizenship, it also *DOES NOT GUARANTEE YOU ADMISSION TO THE UNITED STATES*. Remember: *only* U.S. citizens are guaranteed admission to the U.S. I've personally dumped dozens of green card holders, and I've seen hundreds dumped. In almost every case, the alien excluded would plead, "You have to let me in because I have a green card." But, of course, because the person was an alien and not a U.S. citizen, I didn't have to do any such thing. I dumped 'em anyway, and I dumped 'em gladly.

Green cards have a lot of information printed on them, including the obvious, such as complete name and date of birth. As a traveler trying to beat the border, the one piece of esoteric information listed on a green card which should concern you is the alien registration number (often called just the "A-number"). Everyone on whom the INS keeps a file, including resident aliens, is assigned an A-number. Always, it's an eight-digit code preceded by the letter "A" (for "alien"). A-numbers are listed in this format: A 12 345 678. If you have a green card, it's a wise idea to memorize your A-number. That way, if your card is lost or stolen, the Immigration Service will have a much easier time locating your records. Then you'll get a replacement green card more quickly—but not too quickly. Remember that the INS is a notoriously bureaucratic (and therefore inefficient) bureaucracy.

Security features abound on green cards. Each model (18 to date) has slightly different security features. Pity the poor II who has to memorize all of them. The traveler, however, need only be mindful of two: fingerprint and photo.

If your green card has received rough handling, make certain that the fingerprint has not become smudged or obscured. Perhaps the simplest and surest way an II has of determining that a given green card belongs to the bearer is to take a fingerprint and compare it with the one on the card. Should the print on the card be hard to see, the inspector's suspicions may only be allayed in a more tedious fashion.

Equally important is the photograph of the bearer. Keep that clean and clear. Note especially that photos on green cards always show the bearer's right ear. If you have long hair, the II taking the picture will have you brush it back so that your ear shows. The reason is that no matter how much a person ages, his ear will always look the same (unless cut off or cauliflowered). The shape of the ear is one of the surest means of identification. Hunters of Nazi war criminals, for example, have used the shape of the ear in old photographs to identify people 50 years later.

Always carry your green card on your person if you are a resident alien. If you appear at the border without the card, the INS will charge you a substantial fine (payable only in cash) and admit you only after a lengthy inspection. Getting picked up for something as small as a traffic violation while inside the U.S. without your green card can also get you in trouble with the INS.

The local cops may call the Border Patrol, who will determine your resident status and then fine you. And if you think that the Border Patrol is only on the border, be advised that there are field offices in places like Omaha. The law requires alien residents to carry their green cards at all times, so do it and make life easier for yourself.

A final note about "your" green card. It's not really yours. Forms I-151 and I-551 are, technically, the possessions of the Immigration Service. If you're carrying a worn or mutilated green card, inspectors will tell you to apply for a new one. To ensure that you do it, IIs will write "I-551," or "New Card" into the lamination of your green card. If the II is a real hard case, he'll use a pair of scissors to clip off a corner of your green card, thereby invalidating it for future border crossings. Sometimes, IIs will use the same trick just to cause problems for "LAPRs" ("lappers," from the initials of "lawfully admitted for permanent residence") who piss them off in the course of an inspection. If an inspector does that to you, apply for a new card and wait the months it takes the slow bureaucracy of the INS to supply you with a replacement card before crossing the border. LAPRs without their cards are in trouble: secondary at the very least.

The typical noncitizen traveler doesn't have to worry about green cards, however, because he comes to the U.S. as a nonimmigrant. And the nonimmigrant INS document is the I-94.

You've probably seen an I-94 if you've ever entered the U.S. with a visa in your passport. The I-94 is a piece of white cardboard perforated so that it can be torn into two sections: an "Arrival Record" and a shorter "Departure Record." When an II admits you to the U.S., he'll stamp both parts of the I-94, keep the larger one, and staple the smaller one into your passport.

Theoretically at least, the Arrival Record (with name, date of birth, passport number, visa information, and address in the U.S.) is then sent to an INS computer records center in Kentucky, where the information is put on file and made accessible to IIs at all ports of entry. In fact, however, there are so many I-94s that the information doesn't get into the system for months, long after most visitors have departed. Why the Service persists in using I-

94s as much as it does is beyond me. Bureaucratic inertia is the only explanation.

I've worked at ports where the IIs always filled out the I-94s for the aliens, and I've worked at other ports where the aliens were expected to complete the forms by themselves. If you're at the latter sort of port and you're puzzled by some of the questions (even native English speakers often have difficulty!), don't worry. Look around for samples in your native tongue; most international airports will have a supply printed in French, Spanish, German, Japanese, and other languages. If you can't find those and still need help, ask for it from tour guides, airline personnel, or other travelers. As a last resort, go to the inspector. He may complain while filling out your I-94, but he'll do it. It's his job. When you write your own I-94, be sure to print, and be as neat as possible. It will save time for the inspector and keep him from sending you back to do another. Fill in all the blanks (name, date of birth, etc.) that are obvious, but if in doubt, leave it blank. The inspector can always complete the information if he has to.

On the back of every I-94, there's a warning: ". . . you must surrender it when you leave the U.S. Failure to do so may delay your entry into the U.S. in the future." Frankly, that's bullshit. By all means give up the Departure Record of your I-94 to the appropriate official. But if you forget to do so, don't sweat it. You don't have to mail it to the U.S. embassy or anything like that. On your next trip to the U.S., the II or CI will just remove the old I-94 and write you a new one.

CUSTOMS DOCUMENTS

The USCS doesn't multiply paperwork with quite the enthusiasm of the INS, but it still issues a lot of forms. If you're an importer, ship's captain, or truck driver who crosses the border, you'll have to deal with the more involved documents of the Customs Service. Ordinary travelers, however, usually won't see anything more than a customs declaration.

The kind of advice I gave in regard to I-94s applies equally to customs declarations. Be neat, complete, and honest. U.S.

Customs is generally better-run and more efficient than the INS, and their forms reflect that. The customs declaration is self-explanatory, and you shouldn't have any difficulties in writing it. Clear, clean, and complete "customs decs" will help you to avoid luggage searches and Customs secondaries.

RECORDS

What They Have on You

Do you remember that classic 1960s TV show, *The Prisoner*? The hero was an ex-secret agent trapped in a Kafkaesque place known only as "The Village." When he tried to find out why he was there, the authorities would only say, "We want information, *information*, INFORMATION!"

That response, and indeed the whole show, captured perfectly the mind of bureaucracies and police agencies, including the Immigration Service and U.S. Customs. Inspectors on the border are employed and sworn to seek out information. That's why they'll ask you questions, study your documents, and search your bags whenever you try to cross the border.

More importantly for you as someone interested in crossing the border without being stopped, CIs and IIs have information about you. A lot of information. Inspectors have access to sources of information about criminal records, past crossings, previous exclusions, visas, and many other topics. All that information is a tool with which inspectors can keep you from entering the United States.

This chapter will introduce you to the sources on which inspectors draw. You'll also learn how inspectors use both the information they have on you *and the information they don't have* to dump you.

AN INSPECTOR'S GREATEST WEAPON

Secrecy is an inspector's greatest weapon. As much as what he knows, the fact that *you do not know* what the inspector has on you is a potential way to keep you from crossing the border.

Experienced inspectors will never tell you what they know about you until it's necessary to do so. That's usually when you're being dumped. Even then, a smart inspector will be circumspect.

Let's say, for example, that an inspector suspects you can be dumped for a CIMT. The primary inspector on the line may have been tipped off by any number of factors, from information on his computer lookout system to just the vaguest of hunches. But when he sends you to the secondary inspector, the man on primary will not tell you why he's sending you.

He'll detail his suspicions, usually in code, on a sheet that goes to the secondary inspector. If you, the alien, ask why you're going to secondary, however, the inspector will only give a reply designed to tell you nothing. Often, you'll be referred to secondary with a kind of officialese speech like, "You do not appear readily admissible under the U.S. immigration law, so another inspector will have to ask you a few more questions."

Once you're in secondary, the next inspector won't tell you much more. If he can claim that the office is busy, he'll let you sit and sweat for a while. Worrying about what the inspectors are up to is a useful way of putting an alien off guard for the secondary interrogation.

When the inspector does begin to question you, he may ask the same questions you heard on the primary line: citizenship, place of residence, purpose of trip, and the rest. This tactic serves three purposes. First, it serves to misdirect the alien from the reason he was sent to secondary and throws off any prepared answers he may have ready. Second, it allows the secondary inspector to determine if you're a thorough-going liar who will change your answers from the ones you gave on primary. Third, repeating the same questions tends to make some people angry, and once they've lost their cool, the inspector has an advantage over the alien. In that respect, inspections are like being in the ring: once a fighter loses his cool and starts swinging wildly, the man who keeps his science is the one who'll win almost every time.

Different inspectors will say different things to keep from telling you what they know. Some will use a tough-guy routine: "I don't have to tell you anything." He'll be right about that too, because, as you should always keep in mind, the burden of proof is on you. Some will rely on cryptic bureaucratese. "We have reason to believe . . ." is common. I always liked to say, "I can neither confirm nor deny . . ." If you keep asking "Why? Why? Why?" to even the friendliest inspector, you're liable to hear something like, "I'm the inspector and you're the alien applying for admission to the U.S. I ask the questions and you answer them."

An unwritten rule I was taught by the INS was: never tell the alien anything he doesn't need to know. And as far as IIs are concerned, the alien needs to know damned little. Therefore, keep up your guard if an inspector seems to be telling you too much. He may just be a fool (I certainly worked with more than my share of those when I was an II). Or he may be setting you up for something else. You won't know for sure until the inspection is over and you're either dumped or down the road. Sometimes an alien can't even be sure he's safe when the inspection is over. In the computer lookout system are things called "silent hits." In such cases, the II or CI on the primary line lets the alien travel but then notifies the agency that posted the lookout, such as the DEA, FBI, or Secret Service. That agency then follows the alien in the U.S. without the alien knowing he's under surveillance.

FOREIGN SOURCES

If you think that your criminal record is unknown to the U.S.

Immigration and Naturalization Service and U.S. Customs because all your arrests were in a foreign country, then guess again. Police agencies share information. That fact makes it easy for inspectors on the U.S. border to dump an alien for crimes committed in the alien's own nation.

America's northern neighbor cooperates most closely with the INS and U.S. Customs. Once a Canadian citizen or "landed immigrant" (resident alien) is in secondary at the U.S. border, it's an easy matter for the inspector to determine if the alien has a record. He gets on the phone to the Canadian Police Information Centre (CPIC), identifies himself by name, title, and a code number, and then receives all there is to know about someone's record in Canada.

Neither the Canadian nor the United States government wants you to know that. Officially, that is. On the northern border it's an open secret that the governments share information about criminals. Don't expect an II to admit that fact when he dumps you for a CIMT, however. If asked how he knows about your record in Canada, the inspector will fall back on the usual evasiveness of the Service. "We have reason to believe . . ." After all, the burden of proof is on the alien, not the inspector.

Mexico is another matter. Canadians are the least nationalistic of peoples, but Mexicans tend to be very touchy about their sovereignty, especially in relation to the "gringos." The Mexican authorities sometimes share information about their citizens' criminal activities in big cases, but even that is suspect. Recall that when an American DEA agent was tortured and murdered by Mexican drug dealers, it was done with the help of corrupt Mexican police (who are by no means rare).

U.S. inspectors have access to the criminal records from other countries through Interpol. Contrary to comic books and spy novels, Interpol has nothing to do with enforcement; it deals only in information. No detective from Interpol is ever going to catch anyone, because Interpol has no detectives. But IIs can and will use information obtained from Interpol to dump aliens. I've personally taken part in cases where records provided via fax by Interpol allowed the INS to stop criminals from Germany and

France at the U.S. border. With the growth of international organized crime, border inspectors are using Interpol more and more.

COMPUTER FILES

As if foreign sources weren't enough to make crossing the U.S. border difficult, both the USCS and Immigration Service have extensive sources of their own. When you see an inspector on the line type on a keyboard and look at a computer screen, you can be sure that he's consulting one of those computerized files. They are the most important lookout systems available at the border.

The most widely used system is the Treasury Enforcement Computer System (TECS). Although the system is owned by the Customs Service, both IIs and CIs use it on the primary line wherever dual-inspection is in force. TECS, therefore, contains both customs and immigration lookouts.

At land borders, inspectors find out if you're wanted via the license plate on your car. That's why you'll see CIs and IIs looking intently at your license number, even getting out of the booths to check it, before starting the inspection. TECS can also be used for name checks on primary, especially at airports or with pedestrians at the land border. If an alien comes up wanted, usually due to a prior exclusion, the inspector will refer to him as a "hit" and send him to secondary.

In rare cases, a TECS hit is an "A & D" (for "armed and dangerous"). Being inspected on the line, you probably won't know that you've come up A & D. However, a silent alarm will alert all the other inspectors in the other booths and in the secondary area, who'll come running to the aid of the inspector with the hit. Inspectors know that A & D information in TECS is sometimes suspect or downright erroneous, but they won't take chances. If an inspector orders you to keep your hands on the steering wheel, do it before you get shot. Likewise, if you see your car suddenly surrounded by CIs and IIs, sit still, keep your hands in plain sight, and remain calm.

The INS has its own system comparable to TECS called the National Automated Immigration Lookout System (NAILS).

NAILS may be used by IIs on primary at airports and places where there is no dual inspection, but the system is more often employed during secondary inspections. NAILS is a little more complicated than TECS, but it's very useful to IIs because of the variety of functions and information available in the system. An inspector, for example, can search for information about an alien in NAILS not only by name, but also by date of birth, passport number, and A-number. Of course, the system contains primarily INS lookouts, but NAILS also will have tip-offs from USCS, the State Department, DEA, FBI, the Secret Service, and military intelligence.

Nowadays, many ports of entry have terminals for the Integrated Border Information System (IBIS). The great advantage of IBIS is that it combines the information in TECS and NAILS into one system. IBIS gives inspectors on primary the fullest possible lookout system.

There are a couple of other computer files often used by inspectors during secondary inspections. The first is the Automated Visa Lookout System (AVLOS) of the State Department. This file contains lists of people who should not be granted visas for the U.S. The World Trade Center bombers obtained their visas because some flunky from State misspelled their names at the embassy in Khartoum, so they didn't come up as hits in AVLOS. Lookout systems are only as good as the fools who use them.

The other common system employs the records of the National Crime Information Center (NCIC) run by the FBI. NCIC is used by police all around the U.S. It lists wanted criminals, stolen cars, and suchlike. When a highway patrolman takes your driver's license back to his car, he's usually checking you out with the NCIC terminal on the dashboard. Inspectors on the border use NCIC in about the same way. If you're a hit in TECS, NAILS, or IBIS on the primary line, you can bet that the inspector in secondary is also going to check you against NCIC.

SLOBS AND SOUNDEX

In this age of high-tech police work, the INS still employs a low-tech lookout device, the Service Lookout Book (SLB), better known as the "Slob Book." If you hear one II say to another, "Slob 'em," you're not being insulted. That's just inspector's parlance for checking an alien in the SLB. The Slob Book is used when computers are down or in booths that aren't wired for terminals. It's also a valuable double-check for hits in TECS and NAILS. You'll sometimes see the Slob Book in its thick blue binder sitting on the counter of an INS inspection area.

Information in the Slob Book is indexed by means of the Soundex Code. Soundex gives a number for each surname and groups similar names regardless of spelling. The first letter of a name is not coded, and it is followed by three numbers in Soundex.

According to the Soundex code, six groups of consonants have number equivalents. The following table shows what they are:

Letters	Number Equivalents
b, f, p, v	1
c, g, j, k, q, s, x, z	2
d, t	3
l	4
m, n	5
r	6
not coded	0

Vowels are never coded; neither are the consonants w, h, or y. Double consonants count as one. The rule of Soundex is: first letter + three digits in Soundex. My name "Beaumont," for example, is coded B-553 (i.e., first letter "B" + number equivalents for "m," "n," and "t").

A-240s

Don't worry if you're not a master of Soundex. You don't need to be. Unless you're foolish enough to join the INS (and how could you be after reading this book?), you'll never see the inside of a Slob Book. The only reason I've introduced you to the Soundex code is so that I can tell you about a very dirty trick that inspectors can play on you. That trick involves the infamous A-240.

A-240 is Soundex for "asshole" (i.e., first letter "A" + number equivalents for "s" and "l"). If you cause trouble for an inspector, he may write A-240 on your secondary sheet, and that will be a sign for the secondary inspector to put you through the wringer. It is contrary to Service policy and blatantly illegal to write "A-240" in someone's passport, but inspector's still do it. If you find the code in your passport, get a new one or expect to travel as a marked man. For troublemakers with green cards, inspectors will sometimes put a piece of paper over the card and write "A-240," pressing hard with a pen so that the code shows up not only on the paper but also becomes part of the lamination on the card. The code will then be invisible to the casual eye but apparent to other inspectors—who will do everything in their power to give the bearer of the card a hard time. Again, if you find "A-240" on your I-551, then get a new one.

Better yet, avoid being labeled an A-240 at all. As I've stressed throughout this book, a simple way to beat the border is to make an inspector's job easy for him. Mind your manners.

STAY OFF THE RECORDS AND STAY FREE

For the reader, as someone wanting to cross the border quickly and easily, the point about records to keep in mind is this: stay off them. The sad fact is that once you're in the system, you're probably in for good. Police bureaucracies love information, and they won't willingly part with any of it. Adolf Hitler, you may recall, was still an INS lookout 100 years after his birth and 40 years after he was dead.

Once you're listed on any lookout system, you're liable to run into delays (at least) whenever you try to enter the United States. By following the advice I've given since Chapter 1, however, you should be able to avoid getting into the system and all the related hassles. In short, you should be able to beat the border.

APPENDIX I

What Does My Visa Mean?

The following is a list of visa classifications (letters A through Q), what the classifications mean, and for how long a person may be admitted under that classification.

Class	What It Means	Maximum Period of Admission
A-1	Ambassadors, Diplomats, Heads of State and members of their immediate families	D/S (duration of status)
A-2	Lesser foreign officials, e.g., support and technical staff	D/S

A-3	Servants, butlers, and personal employees of A-1 or A-2	D/S
B-1	Temporary visitor for business (also religious missionaries)	1 year
B-2	Temporary visitor for pleasure (i.e., tourists)	6 months to 1 year
TC	Canadian citizen working under the Free Trade Agreement	1 year
WB	Business visitor admitted under Visa Waiver Pilot Program (citizens from Western Europe and Japan)	90 days
WT	Tourist admitted under program as above	90 days
C-1	Alien in direct and continuous transit through the U.S.	29 days
C-2	Alien in transit to the United Nations headquarters in NYC	D/S at the UN
C-3	Foreign government employees, their families, or servants in transit through the U.S.	29 days
D-1	Crewman (ship or plane) departing on same vessel	29 days

D-2	Crewman departing on different vessel, or aircrew departing on different airline	29 days
E-1	Treaty trader and family	1 year
E-2	Treaty investor (usually someone who has invested $1 million or more) and family	1 year
F-1	Academic student	D/S
F-2	Spouse or child of F-1	D/S
G-1	Resident representative of international organization (e.g., Red Cross, World Bank) and family or personal staff	D/S
G-2	Temporary representative of international organization, and family or servants	D/S
G-3	Representative of nonmember (or nonrecognized by State or the president) country, and family	D/S
G-4	Officer or employee of international organization, and family	D/S
G-5	Servants of G-1 through G-4	3 years
H-1A	Registered nurses	time of employment + 30 days

What Does My Visa Mean?

H-1B	Person working on R&D project for Department of Defense	3 years
H-2A	Temporary agricultural workers	3 years
H-2B	Temporary nonagricultural workers	3 years
H-3	Trainee (agriculture, commerce, communications, finance, government, transportation)	up to 2 years
H-4	Spouse or child of H-1A through H-3	same as principal alien
I	Foreign journalists	D/S
J-1	Exchange visitor (e.g., on Rotary Club exchange program)	time of exchange program + 30 days
J-2	Spouse or child of J-1	same as above
K-1	Fiance or fiancee of USC	90 days
K-2	Child of K-1	90 days
L-1	Intracompany transferee	5-7 years
L-2	Spouse or child of L-1	same as principal
M-1	Vocational student	1 year
M-2	Spouse or child of M-1	same as principal

O-1	Extraordinary ability in science, art education, business, movie and TV stars	3 years
O-2	Accompanying or assisting O-1	3 years
O-3	Spouse or child of O-1 or O-2	same as principal
P-1	Professional athletes and "entertainment groups" (e.g., rock bands)	1 to 5 years
P-2	Reciprocal exchange groups	6 months
P-3	Artists and entertainers in a culturally unique group (e.g., Russian folk dancers)	6 months
P-4	Spouse or children of P-1 through P-3	same as principal
Q	Aliens participating in an "International Cultural Exchange Program"	15 months

As you can see, most of these visas are not the sort of thing the typical traveller is likely to see. Still, it may help to clear up confusion some time.

APPENDIX II

The Old 33

Here are all the old grounds for exclusion. All are part of Section 212(a) of the I & NA. Inspectors will sometimes still use these number as a code among themselves.

1. Mentally retarded
2. Insane
3. One or more attacks of insanity
4. Psychopaths, sexual perverts, mental defects
5. Drug addicts and alcoholics
6. Contagious disease
7. Aliens with physical defects not covered in 1 through 6
8. Paupers, professional beggars, vagrants
9. CIMT (conviction *or* admission)
10. Two or more crimes for which alien was sentenced
    to at least five years

11. Polygamous immigrant
12. Prostitutes, pimps, illegal gamblers
13. Immoral sexual acts (formerly used to dump homosexuals)
14. Immigrants without labor certification
15. Public charge (e.g., an alien on welfare)
16. Excluded and deported within one year
17. Arrested and deported within five years
18. Stowaways
19. Obtained visa or entry via fraud
20. Immigrant without an immigrant visa
21. Immigrant with improperly charged immigrant visa
22. Ineligible to citizenship (draft-dodgers and deserters)
23. Narcotics offense
24. Deleted: this was never enforced and was kept on the list to maintain continuity
25. Illiterate immigrants
26. Nonimmigrant without required passport or visa
27. Prejudicial to U.S. government
28. Communists and anarchists
29. Espionage, sabotage, acts subversive to national security
30. Someone accompanying an excluded alien
31. Alien smuggler
32. Immigrant doctors without U.S. accreditation
33. Nazi war criminals

GLOSSARY

A-240: Inspectors' code for "asshole." Used to label troublesome aliens.

The Act: The Immigration and Nationality Act of 1952. Revised four times, but still the fundamental law of the border. Also called the "INA," the "I&NA," and the "I&N Act."

Alien: Anyone other than a citizen of the United States. Not a pejorative term.

A-Number: Alien registration number given by the INS to anyone on whom it keeps a file. Uses the following format: A 12 345 678.

AVLOS: The Automated Visa Lookout System of the State Department. Lists people who should not be granted visas to the U.S.

CI: Customs Inspector. Pronounced "See Eye."

CIMT: Crime Involving Moral Turpitude. Aliens can be excluded for these crimes. Pronounced as "See Eye Em Tea."

Dual Inspection: System used at most border crossings under which inspectors from one service enforce the laws of both services.

Dump: As a verb, "to dump" is to exclude someone from the U.S. or keep him from crossing the border. Also used as a noun for an alien who has been dumped.

Duty: A tax charged by U.S. Customs on foreign goods imported into the U.S. Most often charged on alcohol and tobacco.

Green card: A wallet-sized immigrant visa. Common term for forms I-151 (old version) and I-551 (new model). Allows an alien to reside in the U.S. but does not grant U.S. citizenship. Therefore, does not guarantee admission to the U.S.

I-94: Ubiquitous nonimmigrant document issued by the INS. Longer top half is an "Arrival Record," and bottom half is a "Departure Record."

IBIS: The Integrated Border Information System. Used as a lookout by inspectors on primary.

II: Immigration Inspector. Pronounce as if saying "yes" in the navy: "aye-aye."

ImmAct 90: Most recent revision of The Act. Rearranged the old 33 exclusions into five categories.

INS: Immigration and Naturalization Service. Part of the Department of Justice. Deals with people at the border and responsible for excluding them.

LAPR: Lawfully Admitted for Permanent Residence. Bearer of a green card. Pronounced "lapper."

NAILS: The National Automated Immigration Lookout System. Computer files of the INS.

NCIC: The National Crime Information Center. Controlled by the FBI. Basic police computer search system.

On the line: Where inspectors perform primary inspections in the rows of booths at border crossings.

Preflight Inspection: Inspection of aliens before they board flights bound for the United States. U.S. government inspection performed in a foreign country.

Primary: First and most basic inspection. Performed on the line. Usually 30 to 60 seconds long.

Secondary: More in-depth inspection that takes place after primary. Both Customs and Immigration perform secondary inspections.

Slob Book: The Service Lookout Book (SLB). Issued by the INS. Contains coded listings of excludable aliens.

TECS: The Treasury Enforcement Computer System. Computer lookout files of the Customs Service.

USCS: United States Customs Service. Part of the Treasury Department. Deals with goods that cross the border.

USPHS: The United States Public Health Service. Uniformed doctors of the USPHS will sometimes perform inspections at border crossings.

Wetback: Originally a term for Mexicans who illegally entered the U.S. by swimming the Rio Grande and thereby got wet. Became in popular speech an insulting term for Mexican-Americans. Used by inspectors to refer to any illegal entrant, regardless of origin. Has no pejorative sense in that context.